WHAT YOUR BOSS REALLY WANTS FROM YOU

Also by Steve Arneson

Bootstrap Leadership

More Praise for *What Your Boss Really Wants from You*

"This book is a must-read for both employees and bosses—filled with practical exercises that will make you, your boss, and your company more successful."

—Helmuth Ludwig, CEO, Siemens Industry Sector

"Steve Arneson understands that while the boss is the team's quarterback, it is teamwork—built on high-caliber interpersonal relationships—that leads to business excellence."

—Steve Swad, CEO, Rosetta Stone

"Steve Arneson reveals a window into your manager's true motives—just what you need to build a successful partnership with your boss."

—Marc Effron, author of *One Page Talent Management* and President, The Talent Strategy Group

"In this fascinating book, Steve Arneson offers a practical road map for understanding and adapting to your boss's motives and style. If you want to improve your relationship with the boss, read this book."

—Bridgette Weitzel, Chief Talent Officer, BAE Systems

"Getting along with your boss is the key to a long, successful, and fulfilling career. In this smart book, Steve Arneson shares his secrets for improving your most critical work relationship."

—Bill Allen, Chief Human Resources Officer, Macy's, Inc.

"This book is an invaluable resource for employees and a smart read for all managers who want to be more open about their style, motives, and values."

—Linda Simon, Senior Vice President, Leadership and Organization Development, DIRECTV

"Managing the relationship with your boss is indispensable for career success; in clear, direct, and punchy prose, Steve Arneson provides explicit and essential advice."

—Robert Hogan, PhD, President, Hogan Assessment Systems

"Steve Arneson takes years of observation and distills it into a simple guide on how to improve your most important work relationship."

—Fred Knowles, Senior Vice President, Human Resources, Under Armour

"Steve Arneson delivers an insightful and practical playbook about the ever-challenging employee-boss relationship with this clever follow-up to *Bootstrap Leadership*."

—David DeFilippo, Chief Learning Officer, BNY Mellon

"Steve Arneson has captured the insights and practical advice needed to build and sustain a powerful relationship with your boss."

—Scott E. Nelson, CEO, MDA Leadership Consulting

"Steve Arneson asks all the right questions to help us understand the boss and motivates us to adapt and take responsibility for the relationship."

—Jane Sommers-Kelly, Managing Director, Duke Corporate Education

"Steve Arneson's book is a must-read for bosses and subordinates who are interested in building more effective professional relationships with each other."

—Boris Groysberg, Richard P. Chapman Professor of Business Administration, Harvard Business School

"This book offers a fresh approach to navigating the relationship with your boss. The process and insight Steve Arneson shares can help you get this critical relationship right."

—Jeff Smith, Global Head of Human Resources, BlackRock

"We've all had at least one challenging boss in our careers, and this book shows you practical ways to take ownership of that relationship to realize your full potential."

—Doug Rose, Chief Human Resources Officer, Discover Financial

"Steve Arneson once again delivers with provocative questions and insights. He provides practical tips for taking accountability and maximizing your most important professional relationship."

—Tim Tobin, Vice President, Global Learning and Leadership Development, Marriott International

"This book is for all those who have ever gotten a knot in their stomach when they get an email or voice mail from their boss. Steve Arneson gives you an effective strategy for the relationship so you'll never feel that anxiety again."

—Jim Norton, Head of Global Media Sales, AOL

WHAT YOUR BOSS REALLY WANTS FROM YOU

15 Insights to Improve Your Relationship

STEVE ARNESON

BK

Berrett–Koehler Publishers, Inc.
San Francisco
a BK Business book

Berrett-Koehler Publishers, Inc.
235 Montgomery Street, Suite 650
San Francisco, CA 94104-2916
Tel: (415) 288-0260 Fax: (415) 362-2512 www.bkconnection.com

Ordering Information

Quantity sales. Special discounts are available on quantity purchases by corporations, associations, and others. For details, contact the "Special Sales Department" at the Berrett-Koehler address above.

Individual sales. Berrett-Koehler publications are available through most bookstores. They can also be ordered directly from Berrett-Koehler: Tel: (800) 929-2929; Fax: (802) 864-7626; www.bkconnection.com

Orders for college textbook/course adoption use. Please contact Berrett-Koehler: Tel: (800) 929-2929; Fax: (802) 864-7626.

Orders by U.S. trade bookstores and wholesalers. Please contact Ingram Publisher Services, Tel: (800) 509-4887; Fax: (800) 838-1149; E-mail: customer.service@ingrampublisherservices.com; or visit www.ingrampublisherservices.com/Ordering for details about electronic ordering.

Printed in the United States of America

Berrett-Koehler books are printed on long-lasting acid-free paper. When it is available, we choose paper that has been manufactured by environmentally responsible processes. These may include using trees grown in sustainable forests, incorporating recycled paper, minimizing chlorine in bleaching, or recycling the energy produced at the paper mill.

Library of Congress Cataloging-in-Publication Data
Arneson, Steve.
What your boss really wants from you : 15 insights to improve your relationship / Steve Arneson.
pages cm
Summary: "A poor relationship with the boss is the leading cause of dissatisfaction at work. Steve Arneson (bestselling author of Bootstrap Leadership, over 11,000 copies sold) says it's time to stop complaining about the boss and take charge of the relationship. When you understand what makes your boss tick, you can begin to put the focus where it belongs: on yourself"—Provided by publisher.
ISBN 978-1-62656-077-2 (pbk.)
1. Managing your boss. 2. Interpersonal relations. 3. Career development.
I. Title.
HF5548.83.A76 2014
650.1'3—dc23

2014005107

First Edition

18 17 16 15 14 10 9 8 7 6 5 4 3 2 1

Cover Design: Irene Morris Design
Text Designer: Detta Penna
Copyeditor: Kathleen Rake, Click Media Works
Indexer: Kirsten Kite
Single key image: © Vincent Giordano | Dreamstime.com
Ring of keys image: © Bagwold | Dreamstime.com

To all of my best bosses –
Thank you for your integrity and honesty

CONTENTS

INTRODUCTION

As an executive coach, I've worked with hundreds of people in all types of organizations, guiding them through a professional development journey. It's a fascinating process, one that has the potential to change their work lives. Each person has their own story, of course—a unique narrative that includes their skills, experience, strengths, weaknesses, and relationships. Yet while every engagement is different, these people all have one thing in common: their boss always plays a central role in the story. That's why my first coaching question is, *What does your boss really want from you?* This is where the reflective process starts because determining what the boss wants is essential to success in any job.

Now, some of my clients have great bosses, so we discuss the relationship briefly and move on to their development opportunities. Great bosses have a lot of wonderful qualities, including a clear picture of what they want from you. They expect you to: 1) have a strong work ethic, 2) demonstrate a positive attitude, 3) be a team player, 4) generate innovative ideas, and 5) get outstanding results. The best bosses clearly express their expectations in these and other areas. They also want what's best for you; they want to see you grow, develop, and succeed.

However, many of my clients don't work for a great boss. They don't understand what he really wants. They're not clear about his expectations. They don't know what he thinks of them, and all this uncertainty impacts their engagement, performance, and happiness. In these cases, we spend as much time talking about the boss as we do discussing their specific improvement opportunities. In fact, for some of my clients, the "boss issue" is the only conversation that really matters.

Hidden Motives

Let me be clear: it's not that these people lack agreed upon objectives. In every case, there are formal performance goals that have been agreed to by the boss. I'm talking about the unknown expectations, those hidden motives that may drive his behavior and the real reasons behind his agenda. Let's face it, some bosses have ulterior motives, and they're certainly not going to share them with you. Do you really know why he approves one project but rejects another? Why he lets you interact with some senior leaders but not others? Why he never lets you make a presentation to his manager? Your boss may have motives that have nothing to do with helping you achieve your goals. Not every boss is like this, of course. Many are perfectly transparent and have clear intentions. But some have motives that don't align with your best interests, and that can cause a lot of sleepless nights.

A Necessary Relationship

There's a good reason for this anxiety, of course. Your boss is the most important person in your work life. He has the power to hire and fire, to empower or micro-manage. He determines (to a large extent) how you'll be recognized and rewarded. He controls whether you get promoted, and how you're thought of by senior management. Now, in a perfect world, all bosses would be skilled managers; all would have pure motives that help you grow, develop, and deliver great results. But the fact is, not all managers are wired this way. That is why you need to know what motivates him. If you don't understand why your boss does what he does, or what he really wants from you, you'll likely be worried, frustrated, and disengaged; you certainly won't be delivering your best work.

The Unexpected Solution

I wish there were an easy solution to this problem. Let's go back to my clients who are struggling with their bosses. The first thing they want to know is, *How do I change my boss?* Know what I tell them? Forget about changing him. That's right, the hard truth is that all of your efforts to improve, fix, or convert your boss won't work. The secret is changing your own approach to interacting with your boss. The "fix" is adapting your own style to make the relationship work. The transformation has to be one you undergo in your awareness, attitude, and behaviors. This isn't always easy, but it's the only path that will get you to a better place with your boss.

What you can't do is continue to play the victim. I've seen a lot of people fall into "victim mode" when it comes to the boss; everything is the boss's fault. These people create a story about the boss that fits their view of the world, and that story generally doesn't reflect reality. Are you doing this? Are you living in a story that doesn't allow you to improve the relationship? If so, my goal is to help you see your boss more objectively, to help you change your story, demonstrate new behaviors, and take charge of the relationship.

How to Use This Book

This is a book about insight. Specifically, it's about turning insight into self-awareness and behavior change. The process described here helps you better understand where your boss is coming from, and provides a roadmap for adjusting your own attitude and behavior to fit his true motives. The book is divided into three sections, and begins by asking you to *Study Your Boss.* The first step in working more effectively with your boss is gaining an understanding of what drives his behavior—developing a clear picture of his work style, leadership brand, and motives. Next, you must *Consider How Your Boss Sees You.* Here you need to draw an accurate picture of how you're perceived by the boss. Studying your boss is important, but you also have to look at yourself from his perspective. Finally, you have to *Take Responsibility for the Relationship*. This is the real key to improving your work life: being accountable for the boss relationship. The first two sections are about gaining awareness; this section is about turning those insights into action. Here you'll find practical suggestions for changing your story, tips for interacting more effectively with your boss, and advice for getting the relationship back on track. In each section, I share examples from my own work experience as well as stories from my coaching practice. All of these examples are real and are meant to illustrate scenarios you may be experiencing right now. Whether you work in a small company (where the boss may be the founder) or a large corporate, government, or educational institution, I think these examples will resonate with you.

Finally, two notes about the purpose and structure of the book: First, while this process is designed for you, I believe bosses can gain valuable insight from the questions as well. The attitude and behavior adjustments don't have to be one-sided. So if you're also a boss, use this book to bring more transparency into your motives and actions; your team will appreciate the effort. Second, most of us have worked for male and female managers. For simplicity, I refer to the boss as a male in Section 1, a female in Section 2, and use both genders in Section 3. However, all of the questions and suggestions in the book apply equally to male and female managers.

Look, I hope you work for a great boss. But even if you do, there may be things about him you don't understand; this process gives you the insight to create an even stronger working partnership. However, if you are struggling with your boss, it might be because you haven't cracked the code of what really motivates him. You haven't figured out what he *really* wants and, therefore, what he wants from you. Most importantly, you haven't made the commitment to change your own attitude and behavior to better align with his style. If that's the case, I believe this book can help you. I hope you'll find this process useful in creating a more meaningful, productive, and enjoyable work experience.

Steve Arneson
Boulder, Colorado

STEP 1

Study Your Boss

Your boss is the central character in your work life. No matter how long you've been working, I bet you can name every boss you ever had—that's how powerful their imprint is on us. We remember our bosses because they have a significant impact on our overall work experience. I've long forgotten most of the details of my first part-time job (which was decades ago) but I'll never forget Mr. Peterson, my first boss. Mr. Peterson was a taskmaster, but he was fair and supportive if you were willing to work hard. I learned a lot from him, most of which went beyond how to do the job. He taught me the meaning of work ethic, commitment, and accountability.

I imagine you have lots of boss stories, too. I bet you could also tell me how each boss made you feel—whether you enjoyed working for them or couldn't wait to get away from them. Whether you loved coming to work or dreaded Monday mornings. Bosses are like that, it seems; we either love them or hate them.

How many bosses will you have in your career? Given that the average U.S. job tenure is 4.1 years (according to the *Bureau of Labor Statistics*) you're probably going to have at least 15–20 different bosses before you retire. What are the odds that every one of them is going to be a great manager? How many will have your best interests in mind? How many will be focused on your growth and development? How many will be comfortable with you being the star? The fact is you're almost certain to work for both good and bad bosses in your career … and how you adapt to these different bosses will have everything to do with your job satisfaction.

Best Boss/Worst Boss

One of the exercises I do with corporate leadership audiences involves having them share their "best" and "worst" boss stories. The room is buzzing with energy when they talk about their favorite manager; everyone has a story about their best boss helping to advance their careers. However, the room gets a lot quieter when they tell the worst boss story. In fact, some people would rather not be reminded of this person at all. But here's what's fascinating about this exercise… nearly everyone has a story to share about a good *and* bad boss; they've all had both experiences.

The "best boss" story has many common themes—good direction, empowerment, feedback, recognition, a mentoring relationship, and plenty of opportunities to grow and develop. Above all, there is clear line of sight to everything the boss is about; you get where they're coming from, and know why they do the things they do. Everything is transparent, logical, and understood; simply put, there's always a solid relationship at the heart of the best boss story. They care about you as an individual, too.

The "worst boss" story is a completely different tale. These stories are filled with poor delegation, lack of empowerment, no recognition or feedback, no coaching or mentoring, and oftentimes, even underhanded behavior. To make matters worse, the worst bosses are hard to read; you never truly know why they do what they do. In fact, when you work for one of these bosses, you feel confused and frustrated a lot of the time; there just isn't a strong relationship, or even the possibility of building one. Bad bosses tend not to care about you as a person.

Why do some bosses care about you while others don't? Why are some bosses open and transparent, while others are closed off or malicious? Why are some bosses confident and egoless, while others are insecure? I think it has everything to do with their personal motives. Everything your boss does (or doesn't do) can be traced back to his beliefs or values—which produce a distinct set of motives. You want to have a better relationship with your boss? It starts with understanding what really drives his behavior.

Understanding Your Boss's Motives

To paraphrase Leo Tolstoy's quote about families, all good bosses resemble each other, but each bad boss is different in their own way. Therein lies the essence of this book—if you're struggling to get along with your boss, you have to figure out his unique motivations. You see, I believe that every behavior can be traced back to a specific motive—that even bad bosses do things for a reason. The problem is the bad boss's motives are often misguided or self-serving. If he doesn't let you meet with his boss, for example, there's a reason for that … and in order to truly understand why, you have to understand his motives.

There is no doubt that our personal motives drive our actions. Some of us are motivated by money, others crave recognition. Some of us just want to do good work; others want to get ahead at all costs. Some of us want to be liked by everyone and others couldn't care less about making friends at work. Some of us are afraid of making a mistake; others are more comfortable with risk. We're all motivated by something ... and that includes your boss.

I wish I could tell you exactly what your boss wants from you. But I'm not in the relationship—you are. So you have to do the work ... you have to study his behaviors to truly understand his motives. The key to working comfortably with your boss is figuring out what drives his thoughts and actions.

Study Your Boss

If your boss is a mystery to you, you need insight. Insight is the understanding of the motivational forces behind one's actions, thoughts, or behavior. This definition perfectly describes what I'm trying to help people achieve through coaching—a clear picture of what is driving their boss's behavior. We do this through a process I call "studying your boss."

I have found that people who struggle with their boss generally haven't done their homework; they haven't rigorously studied their manager's behavior to uncover core motives. They feel the result of the boss's behavior, but don't understand what is causing it. They're frustrated by their interactions with the boss, but they don't know what to do about it. When I work with people who fit this description, I ask them a series of questions to help them gain the insight needed to adjust the relationship with their boss.

This process of studying your boss involves ten questions. Each question is designed to offer awareness into the boss's behaviors or mindset. The answers may come from asking the boss directly, talking with peers, or just paying closer attention to your immediate environment. However gained, the insights will give you a much clearer picture of the underlying motives that drive your boss's actions. At this stage, I just want you to thoughtfully consider and answer these questions as best you can. Try the writing exercises, and reflect on what you've learned. Later, in section three, I'll provide suggestions for adapting to various motives. Here are the questions:

Study Your Boss

Management Style

1. When and how is he most approachable?
2. What is his preferred management style?
3. What behaviors does he reward?

Mission & Priorities

4. What is he trying to accomplish in this role?
5. What is he worried about?

Leadership Brand

6. What is his reputation in the company?

Relationships

7. Whom does he respect?
8. Where does he have influence?
9. What is his relationship like with his boss?

Primary Motivation

10. What is his primary motivation?

As we take a look at each of the questions in depth, write down your thoughts or observations to each question and dig deep for signs or signals that you haven't noticed before. Ask trusted peers for their opinions, and pay attention to your boss's moods, body language, words, and actions. By carefully considering each question, you will develop a series of insights that will help explain his behavior.

❶ When and how is he most approachable?

This seems like a simple question, doesn't it? Yet there is a great deal of insight to be gained by studying when and how to approach your boss. Like all managers, he has a particular style of interacting with his team. Some bosses are informal; you can talk to them anytime, anywhere. Others are more rigid and process oriented. The key is to figure out his preferred interaction style. For instance, can you knock on the door and get a minute of his time? Has he declared his preference about the office pop-in? If not, ask him directly: *Are you open to me coming by your office with a quick question, and if so, when is the best time during the day?* If that doesn't work, ask one of your peers or just pay attention to the pattern of when you've been most successful. I once worked for a boss who literally wouldn't allow the "do you have a minute" request—you had to set up an appointment to ask a simple question. Believe me, I wasted a lot of time and energy before I figured this out, and was getting worried that he didn't like me. But it really had nothing to do with me. It turned out he preferred to read and prepare for any discussion and didn't feel equipped to make decisions in informal conversations (this single insight explained a lot about this boss, by the way).

In today's world, understanding his approachability means knowing when to call, text, or instant message, too. The same principles apply—when is he most approachable, and what are his preferences? Some bosses prefer e-mail over phone calls; others want to talk directly if possible. Some bosses text; others won't. Some bosses are accessible when they are out of the office and others aren't. You get the idea. It's about knowing when and how. But it's also about knowing why.

Understanding why is what helps you make sense of his

behavior. I recently coached Tanya, who was experiencing a huge disconnect with her boss. She kept trying to call him directly, and the boss always refused to take her call; the boss's assistant would just say, "Send him an e-mail." And of course, whenever Tanya did that, she received a prompt, thoughtful reply. Strange, I know. Wouldn't it be quicker to just talk on the phone? Of course, the boss never explained his motive, which drove Tanya crazy; she was convinced the boss thought she was a poor performer. Now, as it happens, in my feedback process, I learned the boss wanted a written record of every interaction. He didn't like the phone for even the shortest conversations because it didn't allow for a trail of detail or evidence. Was the boss anti-social? Almost certainly. But the real motive behind his interaction style had nothing to do with that; rather, it was based in a more practical (some would say paranoid) reason. This is a perfect example of the value of digging deep to gain an understanding of the core motives behind your boss's behavior. The "why" isn't always what it seems to be, and much of the time, it isn't about you at all.

The second thing you need to study is his mood pattern. What puts him in a good mood, or conversely, a bad frame of mind? What day of the week is he most approachable? When should you leave him alone? Is he stressed right before a meeting with his boss? Do certain events or deadlines impact his approachability? Try this exercise: For a month, make a daily diary of his moods. Name the mood (angry, happy, sad, etc.) and note how approachable he was each day. Then, study the diary to learn your boss's patterns and work around them to your advantage.

Third, how much can you challenge your boss in group settings? What style of interaction works best? Is he open to rigorous debate? Most managers hold staff meetings with their direct reports, and there are unwritten rules about challenging the boss's ideas, how long to debate an issue in front of the team, etc. Do you know where this line is with your boss? Have you ever crossed it?

A lot of bosses are resistant to anyone disagreeing with them in public, and it can take a while to learn that. One of my clients, Craig, was getting frustrated with his boss's staff meetings because no one would challenge the boss's ideas. As Craig tried repeatedly to push back on his boss (with respect), he made things worse for himself because the boss didn't tolerate or appreciate this interaction style. Craig learned to discuss these issues outside of the meeting format, but it took some reflection about the boss's motives to recognize and make this shift in his approach. The trick is to pay attention to the small signs if you find yourself in a non-productive public conversation with your boss. How is he reacting to you? Study his body language and tone of voice. If you're pushing his buttons, find a gracious exit to the discussion.

Finally, you have to know what subjects are either allowed or out-of-bounds for your boss. What are the topics or questions you can raise, and what are the sacred cows? Where can you probe, and what should you leave alone? There are some issues you shouldn't approach him about; and if you do, he won't talk about them anyway. For years, I tried to get a boss to talk about his life outside of work. He wouldn't do it. I'm an open person, so I thought that was odd—why wouldn't he share what he did on the weekend? It was really bugging me. He would talk about sports and current events, but not about his hobbies or family. Finally, I realized I wasn't going to break through that wall between work and home, and stopped asking him. I accepted that I wasn't going to change him. If he wanted to keep certain things private, that was his choice; he didn't have to be just like me. And you know what? Once I stopped worrying about it, our relationship improved.

The bottom line is that you need to be thoughtful about approaching your boss. He wants you to fit his interaction practices, not create new ones. Every time you push him out of his comfort zone, you risk annoying him. How many minor irritations are you willing to add to your ledger? The easier path is to adapt to his style by learning exactly when and how he is most approachable. Then, work out the rationale for his preferences so you understand where he's coming from; there might be an underlying (albeit quirky) reason that has nothing to do with you. You may not like it, but at least you'll understand it.

INSIGHTS

Approachability

- *Recognize when and how he is most approachable.*
- *Determine how to interact with him in a group setting.*
- *Know what he will and won't discuss with you.*

Combine all of this knowledge to choose the best interaction plan.

❷ What is his preferred management style?

Every boss has their own cadence and rhythm when it comes to getting work done; your job is to figure out what it is, and adapt to it. For example, does your boss like detailed work plans? Does he seek a lot of input before making a decision? Does he like to be hands-on when developing the presentation that goes to his peers and boss? Does he like to work one-on-one with you on a task, or does he pull in members of your team? In short, what's the predictable pattern from start to finish on projects? How does he manage the day-to-day work that goes on in your department?

In my experience, bosses will have a preferred style for at least three basic work tasks. First, they will follow a set process for generating ideas. Some bosses prefer brainstorming; others want to generate their own list of ideas and have you react. Some bosses don't engage much in this phase; they merely want to hear the ideas and then approve a final course of action. Do you know how your boss likes to generate and approve ideas, and why? Make a list of your recent ideas and how your boss reacted to each one. This insight will tell you a lot about him—how much does he want to be involved in this first step of the process?

Most likely, he wants to be involved in solving just certain problems, but couldn't care less about others. This is the proverbial "deep dive" question: how deep into the process will he get, and why? This is one of the most common complaints I hear from clients; they don't know why their boss "goes deep" on one topic, but not another. Oftentimes, there doesn't seem to be a set pattern. It's hard to predict which topic will cause him to get highly engaged. I can assure you it's not random; there's a reason that some issues get his full attention and others don't. More often than not, it has to do with ego or reputation. Your boss's deep dives are generally motivated by a feeling that his solution is clearly the best option, or by not wanting to appear out of touch with the details of important projects.

The second management process to study is his preference for building a presentation. If an idea, proposal, or recommendation needs to be packaged into a story, he is going to have an established method for overseeing this process. Do you recognize all the phases of this work flow? Can you articulate them step-by-step? My guess is that your boss likes to build the business case in a predictable fashion. Your job is to pay attention to his preferences so you can get through the process as efficiently as possible.

Mary is struggling with this right now. She's frustrated by her boss's iterative process for creating a presentation. They go through multiple drafts before arriving at the final version. These iterations change only slightly from one draft to the next, and the boss is heavily involved in reviewing every draft. Mary would like to create a final version without all the review meetings with her boss. When I asked her why the boss preferred to work this way, she answered: "Because he doesn't trust me to develop the story on my own." I encouraged Mary to check this impression with her peers, and what she heard back surprised her. Her colleagues told her the boss liked to check in with his peers on all recommended courses of action, and that he used an iterative process to socialize the proposal, thereby ensuring a greater chance of success. It wasn't that the boss didn't trust Mary; this was just his preferred process for developing a solid recommendation. If your boss likes to work with you on big presentations and likes to evolve the story over time, think about why he's doing this. It might not have anything to do with you.

The biggest area in which you'll encounter your boss's preferred management style is on the day-to-day execution of projects. After the solution has been generated and socialized, the product or service needs to be implemented. Most bosses have distinct opinions about execution and want to be involved in this process, too. Some like to manage the work closely, with lots of update meetings. Others avoid the details, focusing instead on the overall outcome and customer reaction. How does he like to stay engaged during execution? Again, write out his preferences for different scenarios. Some bosses want to read reports; others want to be briefed periodically. Some want these briefings presented in the staff meeting, while others will schedule regular one-on-one sessions.

Know your boss's preferred style of staying up to speed, figure out why he's working from this style, and adapt to it. Don't spend a lot of energy trying to change his style to fit yours: If he likes data-heavy updates, be prepared. If he wants a lot of context, provide it. If you know he favors certain metrics, highlight them. Above all, be calm and flexible because this is your boss's style of managing the work, and you're not going to radically change it.

When the Boss's Style Doesn't Fit

When I starting coaching Melanie, I was surprised by the feedback I collected from her stakeholders. Direct reports loved her, peers admired her, and customers valued her results. So why did she need an executive coach? Because her boss thought she needed to change her approach to navigating the organization. Melanie's style was to experiment with ideas, to be bold and innovative. She was outgoing and wasn't afraid to push the company into new areas. Her boss had a different style; in fact, in my interview with him, he told me that Melanie needed to be "more like me." Specifically, he thought the way to "survive" in the company was to keep your head down, be deferential toward the senior team, and avoid risks. Reflecting on the feedback, Melanie could see where her boss's career advice was coming from—a perspective of "my way is the only way." In the end, Melanie chose to maintain the style that had been working for her. But she did change her approach toward her boss. She chose to respectfully challenge his point of view, rather than simply ignoring it. First, she shared her feedback with him, so he could see how the rest of the organization viewed her. Second, she began offering alternative viewpoints whenever he provided career guidance (discussing advice as just one way of looking at the world). Finally, she told him she was going to start working with one of the senior team members in a mentoring relationship. Melanie couldn't change her boss's style or even his world view, but she did change how it impacted her.

Finally, a big part of these common management situations involves decision-making.

Do you know his decision-making process? Does he like a lot of data, or does he make decisions with his gut? Does he make decisions quickly, or is it a drawn-out affair? Before making a decision, does he ask a lot of questions? There's really no excuse for missing the consistent patterns of his decision-making style. The trick here is to study his past decisions to determine what will be required on the current business issue. If it's a decision that impacts your group only, perhaps you just need a convincing business case. But if the decision has broader organizational impact, be aware that his decision will be influenced by far more than just the supporting evidence. His peer relationships, his current standing with his boss, his recent track record of making the right call—all of this will come into play. Most of his decisions will not be black or white; instead, they will be highly dependent on the current vibe in the organization. Learn the overall context so you can make sense of his final decision.

Over time, your boss has dug a deep groove in his routine

for managing work. The behavior is there to be observed; you just need to look deeper to understand why he does what he does. From idea to execution, how does he want to be involved? How does he want to be updated? How and why does he make decisions? Observe the behavior and consider the situation, and you'll start to recognize the patterns. Once you can predict the *what* and *why*, it's up to you to make the right adjustments to his style.

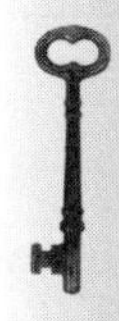

INSIGHTS

Management Style

- *Know how he wants to be engaged in the idea phase.*
- *Be aware of his ongoing engagement style during execution.*
- *Learn his decision-making process.*

Operate within your boss's preferred work style.

❸ What behaviors does he reward?

Just like anyone else, your boss values some behaviors more than others. When it comes to your work style or behavior, do you know what he likes and doesn't like? This insight is critical to establishing a good working relationship. Obviously, if you're doing things that annoy him, that's not going to create a solid foundation. You need to learn his preferences and try to work within those boundaries. Yes, that might mean adapting your style a bit, but if you want to improve the relationship, you need to figure out what he wants from you, and make adjustments.

For example, how does he feel about being on time for meetings? Is it acceptable to call and ask for more time on an assignment? Does he like you to run ideas by him, or does he let you make decisions? Does he want to know where you are throughout the day? Does he want you to e-mail back immediately, or do you have until the end of the day? How does he feel about you working from home? Does he want you to stay in touch when you're on vacation? What does he think of your work space?

These may seem like trivial examples, but I've seen every one of these become a big issue. There are dozens of boss preferences you have to learn, from presentation routines and travel habits to meeting behavior and clothing styles. The problem is, your boss won't always say, *This is a big deal to me*—and often, he wants you to figure it out. So if he gets annoyed by late arrivals, be on time for the meeting (in that exact moment, this is what your boss wants from you). If he likes immediate e-mail replies, respond to his question as soon as possible. If he tells you, *Don't even think about the office while you're on vacation* (but you know he doesn't really mean it), trust your instincts and check in occasionally.

I see this "preferences disconnect" all the time in my

coaching practice. I worked with Harriet, who had arranged to start work early in the morning, allowing her to leave at 4:00 p.m. The boss agreed to this arrangement, even though the rest of the team worked a more traditional work schedule. Sure enough, when I was collecting feedback, the boss told me he was concerned about Harriet's habit of leaving early. This is a perfect example of the boss using preferences to judge performance (in this case, favoring people who stayed late). The hours and output were the same, but he was having a difficult time overcoming his own biases. The only recourse for Harriet was to remind him of their agreement and prompt him to stay open-minded about his commitment. But she has to stay alert to his mood on this issue, and be proactive about addressing it.

Another example is Robert, whose boss insisted he copy him on all e-mails sent to any VP (and above) in the organization. The explanation had something to do with "alignment" or "mission clarity" but the underlying reason was pure paranoia. The boss was a control freak and afraid of being left out of the loop. Robert tried to reason with the boss, but wasn't successful—this was his standing e-mail edict. So Robert had two choices: find another role in the company, or learn to live with this relatively minor annoyance. He chose to live with it, and eventually established his own credibility with his boss's peers.

Of course, the flip side of what he prefers is what he doesn't want you doing. Developing a close relationship with one of his peers is often frowned upon. Some bosses don't want you to speak to their boss without them in the room. Others don't want you asking questions in all-hands meetings or volunteering for extra work around the company. Some bosses don't want you going to industry events; others don't want you becoming a known player in your field. Frankly, there are just as many "don'ts" as there are "do's" when it comes to what behavior your boss wants from you. The bottom line is that you have to learn both the positive and negative preferences—what he tends to reward and what he disapproves of—in order to truly understand his attitude or actions. I recommend making a do-and-don't list and checking it with a trusted peer. Don't get hung up on whether these preferences are right or wrong, or logical or paranoid. Oftentimes they are just minor irritations, but if you ignore them, they can turn into bigger issues for you.

My advice is to study the results, not just the stated direction. In other words, trust what you see, not what he says. Study how he rewards or punishes certain behaviors, and you'll learn his preferences. Pay attention to what happens to people who meet or miss those preferences. Don't ignore the clear signs or clues out there; he is sending dozens of signals each day about what he wants from you. All you have to do is raise your level of awareness and react in a way that best serves your overall goal, which is improving the relationship.

INSIGHTS

Rewarded Behaviors

- *Learn what behaviors are acceptable to your boss.*
- *Know what behaviors are unacceptable.*
- *Be aware of the consequences for out-of-bounds behavior.*

Stick to behaviors your boss finds acceptable.

❹ What is he trying to accomplish in this role?

If your boss is any good at all, he has an agenda; he's trying to accomplish something big in his role. This is a good thing; you want him to have a vision for the department. If that vision aligns with yours, everything's great. But sometimes his mission is hard to interpret and that's when you need to dig deep to study his true intent.

Start by determining his philosophical views about your function or discipline. How does he see the field? Which experts does he respect and follow? Is he a traditionalist, or does he want to take the function in a new direction? Get a fix on how your boss looks at his profession. Once you know his point of view, determine how it aligns with yours. Do you share the same beliefs about the future of your chosen field?

Amanda is an expert in software development, and was struggling with her boss about the approach to take in developing new products. To clear the air, I brokered a meeting between Amanda and her boss that focused exclusively on their philosophical visions. By taking the conversation up a notch to their broader world views, we were able to find some common connection points. When it comes to interpreting the moves your boss is making, it's important to first understand how he sees his craft; this will explain a lot of his initiatives and behavior.

The second thing you should study is his mandate, as you perceive it. Given his philosophical view of the profession and the challenges facing your organization, what is he trying to accomplish in this role? What's his mission? Most great leaders want to make their mark; they want to do something meaningful. How would you articulate his main objective? Write it out as a statement: "In this role, my boss is trying to ___."

Keeping Up With the CEO

Mark was the head of Sales at a start-up company, and when promoted, he was the third sales leader in 18 months. His feedback indicated that he needed to demonstrate more executive presence and decisiveness. In fact, Mark's biggest issue was his boss, the CEO, who also happened to be the founder. Because the CEO had once been a highly successful head of Sales, Mark was getting a lot of "help" from him. The CEO was constantly bombarding Mark with ideas, suggestions, and changes of direction. I'll admit that at first, Mark and I struggled to plot a course of action; after all, how do you tell the CEO/Founder to stop providing input? After we articulated the CEO's motives (a strong desire to "run" Sales), we crafted a three-pronged strategy: 1) Mark significantly increased his updates to the CEO, particularly decisions; 2) he adopted a calming mindset of *I'm the head of Sales until I'm not*—a simple mantra that represented the confidence and presence he needed to convey in order to handle the CEO's style; and 3) he insisted on a weekly meeting with the CEO to prioritize the flow of ideas and direction. By staying calm, being proactive, and forcing the prioritization of work, Mark enhanced his stature with the boss, *not* by changing the boss, but by taking responsibility for the relationship.

Once you've got a sense for it, ask for validation. Force a clear understanding of what he's trying to accomplish by asking: *How would you describe what you're trying to do in this role?* This is one time I recommend seeking direct clarification with your boss. Chances are, he's proud of the mission and will want to share it. The motives behind the mission will be based on his philosophical view and the current organizational challenges, and you need to know what this mission will require of you.

Finally, you need to figure out where you can impact the strategic direction. If your views differ from his, where and how can you influence and shape his world view? What's the best way to debate or discuss an alternative course of action? Juan faced this challenge with his boss, who was the head of Human Resources. Juan was the director of talent management, but was unable to come to agreement with his boss on the subject of high-potential talent. In this case, the boss didn't believe in telling high-potential leaders they were top talent; he believed in keeping the list a secret. Juan held the opposite view just as strongly; he believed top-talent leaders should be told they were being groomed for higher levels. By probing the origins of this belief, Juan learned the boss had had a bad experience in his previous company with publicizing the high-potential list, and was reluctant to try it again. Once Juan understood his influencing obstacle, he built a strong case for why things would be different in their current organization.

Figuring out how your boss sees your profession is an important step to figuring out his behavior. Your boss is going to chart a very specific course when it comes to executing his role. He is grounded in a particular world view and is on a mission to accomplish a specific set of goals. Your job is to study both to determine how you best fit into those plans.

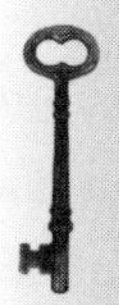

INSIGHTS

Objectives

- *Learn his philosophical views on the function.*
- *Know how he views his role's mission.*
- *Determine if there is tolerance for opposing views.*

Know your boss's views on your function and his mission.

❺ What is he worried about?

Believe it or not, your boss is worried—about something. He wouldn't be human if he weren't experiencing some stress at work. Do you know what it is? Is it a late deliverable? Is it a peer relationship? Is it a budget issue? Is he getting pressure from his boss? I guarantee something is at the top of his priority list, and you'd better know what it is, because that's what he's focused on right now.

Your boss's priorities are the most transparent signal you'll get about what he wants from you. Most bosses are pretty clear about their top priorities, and if they're not, all you have to do is notice how they spend their time. If you can't even get ten minutes with him, he's probably focused on something important. If you're not involved with this priority, what he wants from you is to leave him alone. Pestering him to look at your presentation, or bugging him to get on his calendar is only going to annoy him. To get a handle on what he's concerned about, study his deliverables. Focus on his objectives, what he's promised the organization, his deadlines, etc. The more you know about his commitments, the better. Again, if you need clarification, ask him directly.

Next, figure out what's at the top of his immediate to-do list. What is he most focused on this week? When is it due? Anticipate what (if anything) he might need from you to meet his commitments. I can remember several of my bosses retreating into their bunker to meet a tight deadline or putting in long hours with teams of people; sometimes I was part of that and sometimes I wasn't. During those events, what my boss wanted from me was either total commitment or complete independence. If I wasn't part of what he was focused on in that moment, my best strategy was to stay off his radar screen. Be sensitive to what he's currently involved in, and if it's not something in your area, give him lots of space. Of course if you are involved, he wants you "all in" until the project is finished—what he wants from you right now is total dedication and commitment.

That's good advice for deliverables and work priorities, but what if he's worried about something else? Maybe he's in a sticky situation with a peer, or maybe he's done something to upset his manager (hey, bosses make mistakes, too). Maybe he's getting ready to fire someone and is upset about the circumstances. Maybe he just lost a big battle on the senior team and is worried about losing power, or perhaps it's a personal issue completely unrelated to work.

The fact is your boss experiences all kinds of stress. That's why you need to be aware of his demeanor at all times. If he's normally approachable, and suddenly becomes quiet and unavailable, there's a good chance something is wrong. Pay attention to his moods and body language. Read the behavior change: Is it a work-related issue or is it personal? Is it something serious, or have you seen him pass through this stage quickly in the past? Is it something you can help with, or is it best not to approach him about it?

Scott is experiencing this right now. His boss has gone into a shell and no one can figure out why. He's normally very engaged with his staff, but lately he spends a lot of time behind closed doors. Usually, he's the last one to leave, but recently he's been leaving at 5:00 p.m. Scott has asked if he can help, but the boss has not confided in him. His behavior is impacting the entire department, but at this point, all Scott can do is continue to offer support. I advised Scott to look for things to take off his boss's plate, identifying and completing tasks the boss would have performed normally. Even though he's probably not aware of it, what the boss wants from Scott right now is for him to step up and do more while he's working through his issues.

Here's what I want you to take away from this question: Bosses are human, too. Your boss's motives may involve things you never thought of, like tension or anxiety. A lot of bosses do crazy things when they're under stress, so pay attention to the external forces that may be causing your boss's behavior to shift. What he's worried about (and how he's reacting to it) may be the insight you need to adjust your approach or lend a helping hand.

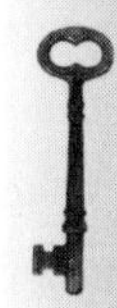

INSIGHTS

Deliverables

- *Know his key deliverables.*
- *Identify what he's most worried about.*
- *Recognize his current priority list.*

Always know your boss's priorities.

❻ What is his reputation in the company?

This is a question that should be easy to answer, because it's mostly an exercise in observation. Trust your eyes and ears to draw the insights you need about your boss's reputation across the organization. Start with the basics—do people feel comfortable around him? Read the body language in meetings. Is there an easy dialogue, or are people afraid of him? Notice how he spends his time. Does he stay in his office, or is he out meeting with different groups? Pay attention to how he talks about other people, and how others talk about him. Is there a measure of mutual respect? Study what conversations he's part of; is he being included in big decisions? Listen to what others are saying to *you* about him—do they envy or feel sorry for you?

The fact is your boss has a leadership brand, and it's well known throughout the organization. His brand is how other people think about him or describe him; essentially, it's his reputation in the company. So how is he perceived? Is he thought of as strategic, creative, or flexible? Is he seen as tactical, uninspiring, or stubborn? Do people trust him? Is he seen as a thought leader in the organization? Are his technical skills well respected? How about his people-management skills? What do people think of his background and qualifications for the role? What do they think of his results? Is his stock rising or falling in the organization?

When studying his leadership brand, try to construct an honest and accurate picture. From my years as an executive coach, I know that leadership brands are generally described in five or six traits; that's all it takes for others to define a reputation. For example, Serena got the following feedback about her brand: strategic, results-oriented, fair, passionate, customer-oriented, and trustworthy. James received this feedback: tactical, cautious, unorganized, self-centered, micro-manager. Which brand would you rather have? The fact is we all have a brand or reputation inside an organization. So what's your boss's leadership brand? Give it some thought, and write it out in six traits or characteristics. Check your list with a trusted peer. Do they agree? Is this how your boss is perceived by others?

This is important for two reasons: First, your boss's leadership brand impacts how people view your whole department. If he's collaborative and easy to work with, that makes life easier for all of you. However, if he has a reputation for being hard to get along with, that can affect your whole team. I once worked for a boss who steadily lowered the influence our whole department had across the organization. When he joined the firm, we were one of the most respected groups in the company. Four years later, we were mostly ignored. The only change on our team was the leader, who, over time, had made enemies or lost support from his boss, and this trickled down to the rest of us. His reputation became the department's reputation, and all of us had a much harder time doing business across the company as a result.

Second, when people don't respect your boss, you suffer personally, too. For instance, if he isn't well thought of, you may not be in the conversation for spot bonuses or rewards because no one is paying attention to your department. You may not be nominated for stretch assignments or promotions if he doesn't have a strong voice at the table. Without support at the talent review or performance management meeting, you're going to see fewer development opportunities, lower raises, or a smaller year-end bonus. I've had several clients who have experienced this; they've seen their peers move more quickly through the organization, mostly because they had a better sponsor. Simply put, these other boss's opinions and support carried more weight, and my clients suffered because they didn't have a well-respected champion. Trust me, this is real; your boss's reputation casts a long shadow over your department, and over you personally.

Managing the Boss's Reputation

When Felicia began her new job as Director of Finance within a government agency, she was impressed with both her boss's knowledge of the agency and his vision for the division. John seemed like the kind of manager she could learn from and one who would help her build relationships across the government's spectrum of clients. She soon discovered, however, that John had a poor reputation as a finance leader; his group had issues with accuracy and meeting commitments. Apparently, there had been a few financial misstatements in the past, and the group's track record of delivering results was considered subpar by other agencies. When I began working with Felicia, this was a major obstacle she wanted to overcome; she knew her reputation would be tied to John's if she didn't act fast. We developed a three-part plan: 1) she worked to change perceptions of John by citing positive examples of his contributions every time she met with her peers; 2) she consistently asked for feedback on herself and the agency as a whole, which made others feel they were being heard. She fed that back to John and the team, which helped them formulate strategies to correct their collective reputation; and 3) she promised (and met) a relentless commitment to accuracy, thereby establishing a new track record of results. This had the effect of growing her brand, but also helped to repair John's reputation of running a solid Finance division.

Once you have an accurate description of his leadership brand, look for ways to make adjustments. Perhaps you need to be defending him more, or maybe you should start defending him less. Start repairing relationships with other leaders and teams. Step up your own networking efforts and seek out a mentor in other areas of the company. Raise your own visibility across the organization so other leaders are familiar with your skills and expertise. The bottom line is this: his reputation can help you or hurt you. If his leadership brand isn't what it should be, start making plans to strengthen your own.

INSIGHTS

Reputation

- *Know his reputation across the company.*
- *Recognize how his brand impacts your department.*
- *Determine what his reputation means for you.*

Be aware of your boss's leadership brand.

❼ Whom does he respect?

The answers to this question contain a lot of insight because they tell the story of where your boss is building (or avoiding) relationships around the organization. All bosses want to work with people they consider capable and talented, and most won't develop strong relationships with colleagues they don't respect. So, what does your boss think of other leaders in the company? Whom does he respect? Whom does he *not* want to work with, because he doesn't respect their style, experience, or outcomes?

Respect is a strong word in business. It means there is something about you that I appreciate, admire, or want to emulate; it's really the highest form of corporate flattery. Given that it's so important, your boss will likely be transparent about whom he respects in the company. He might say, *I have a lot of respect for Bill; he does things the right way.* He may also indicate whom he does not respect. He might tell you directly or it may be apparent in his body language or lack of interaction with that individual.

This knowledge is important to you for several reasons. First of all, it tells you *what* he respects. It's a window into what he values in terms of skills, experience, or work ethic. If you pay attention to what he respects in others, you'll have a good idea of what he wants to see in you. For example, if he respects people who build a broad network, he's sending a signal that he'd like you to develop cross-functional relationships. If he respects people who challenge the status quo, he's giving you license to push back on some of his ideas. If he values a wide range of past experiences, that's a sign that you can reference your previous company's best practices in conversations. Make a list of the qualities your boss respects—this is his set of people "values" and you need to know these basic principles.

Second, you also need to know who he thinks is worthy of his time and attention. His relationships are based on the foundation of respect. Study his relationships and alliances throughout the company. It's highly unlikely that he's going to be close to someone he doesn't respect. Who does he think is talented? Whom does he go to for advice? Whom does he confide in or admire? Whom does he form coalitions with to get work done? Conversely, who does he think is just taking up space? Whom does he avoid? Whom is he not spending time with, and why?

One of the exercises I do with clients brings this network of relationships to life. On a single page (I call it a Relationship Map), I ask them to plot the quality of their relationships across the company using a simple five-point scale (with anchors of Excellent, Very Good, OK, Needs Improvement, and Poor). While this information is valuable to us in the coaching process, what people really find interesting is when I have them map their boss's relationships. The act of plotting his network reveals a lot, from how he gets work done to where he has blind spots across the company. Try this exercise and rate your boss's relationships across the organization. By analyzing his relationships, you'll get an idea of how he works the system and where he has solid footing on the leadership paths of the organization.

Finally, knowing what and whom he respects gives you a roadmap to navigate the organization; knowing his network is critical to your own relationship-building efforts. For instance, you can leverage his best relationships to accomplish your objectives. You can also use his network to accelerate your ideas and sphere of influence. You may even take on the challenge of building a bridge to a team where he's given up on that group's leader.

Another way to use this knowledge is to understand where the "respect lines" are drawn between you and your boss. Sallie has learned this the hard way. At times, she's criticized one of her boss's colleagues without realizing they were close friends. At other times, she's talked glowingly about a peer that he doesn't respect, which causes him to question Sallie's judgment. Sallie and I have discussed that she doesn't have to adopt his views on people; she's allowed to form her own opinions of others. However, Sallie now understands she needs to be aware of whom her boss admires or doesn't respect.

If you're facing this type of misalignment, you need to figure out how to cope with it because you're not likely to change his deeply held views on people. Know his people values. Be aware of his opinions of the talent in the organization. Know whom he admires and respects. Study his relationships, and know where they're strong or weak. One of the most critical things you can know about him is what he thinks of his colleagues, and where he has strong (or broken) alliances. Armed with this information, you can more accurately predict what he wants from you when it comes to building or leveraging relationships.

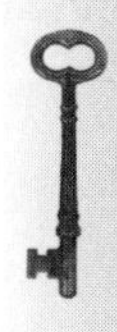

INSIGHTS

Values & Relationships

- *Learn what he values in others.*
- *Know whom he does and doesn't respect, and why.*
- *Realize what these opinions mean for you.*

Know whom your boss respects and why.

8 Where does he have influence?

At first glance, it might seem that studying your boss's reputation and level of influence would yield the same insights. Actually, they're quite different. He might have a reputation as a difficult colleague to work with, but that doesn't mean he can't have impact across the organization. Reputation has to do with people's perceptions; influence has to do with getting things done. Influence is gained by demonstrating a track record of success, having great ideas, and being able to execute. So, does your boss have influence? Does he have the power to get people to do what he wants? Is he a thought leader in the company?

Your homework assignment for this question involves two insights: 1) with whom does he have influence, and 2) what issues or decisions does he successfully impact? Let's start with the senior managers he's able to influence. Look at his track record and consider his success and failures. Is there a pattern? Does he have more success with male peers than female colleagues? Does he have more sway with new leaders or long-tenured executives? Does he have more influence with line leaders or staff leaders? Does he have impact in the field, or is it mostly in the home office? Take the relationship map that you created for question seven in Step 1 and highlight those leaders your boss tends to successfully influence. Where are they in the organization? What do they have in common? Is there any way to help him expand this list?

Ahmad is facing this exact situation. He works in Information Technology, and while his boss has no trouble influencing other staff leaders, he's failed many times to influence business leaders to try new product or service offerings. The boss has the respect of the other staff groups, but hasn't proven himself with the line executives. As it happens, Ahmad came from the major line of business, so he's working to establish his boss's reputation with that group through regular conversations with the leadership team.

In the Line of Fire

Jason was a newly promoted VP in Technology Operations; his knowledge and skills were highly respected, but he needed experience in collaborating and negotiating with internal clients. Unfortunately, Jason's boss wasn't providing much coaching in this area. In fact, Jason's boss avoided conflict with the organization at all costs, and wasn't effective at brokering solutions if Jason escalated issues. One day, Jason told me his boss was putting him in an uncomfortable position with one of the boss's peers. In effect, he wanted Jason to fight his battles for him. The boss was deflecting any responsibility for a project slow-down, and told his peer to "Take it up with Jason." Jason handled this incident with patience and grace, but was frustrated by his boss's total lack of accountability. The key insight came from the senior leaders that Jason ended up working with; apparently, Jason's boss had lost some major debates in the last year and had become reluctant to take a stand on controversial issues. They suspected his plan was to push responsibility down the line. That way, if things weren't resolved, he had someone to blame. Jason suspected that was the correct motive, so together we crafted a strategy where he would get his boss's input before engaging with others across the company. Eventually, Jason learned to work around his boss's inability to confront others, and in the process gained a reputation as a mature business partner who could be counted on for win-win solutions. In the end, Jason turned a negative into a positive, but only after determining his boss's true motive.

The second insight involves the type of issue or decision he typically impacts. Is it just what's in his functional domain, or does he have influence beyond his area of expertise? Are they small issues, or can he make things happen on big organizational challenges? Make a list of the issues or decisions he's able to influence. What stands out for you? As you consider his track record, would you say he's a major player in the company, or is he merely performing his specific functional duties?

While his reputation and ability to influence might yield different insights, the implications for you are similar. If he has power in the organization, then that bodes well for you (a rising tide lifts all boats when it comes to organizational influence). If he doesn't have much influence, you may have trouble getting traction, too. If he's not driving a lot of decisions, there are a couple of things you can do. First, help him get some quick wins by finding an issue that needs his input. Pave the way with your contacts, and put him in position to influence the decision. Second, try to get more involved with your department or company's strategy development process. Again, use your relationships to determine where your group can have greater impact, and steer your boss to a place where he can add the most value.

Your boss's ability to influence the organization affects his confidence, attitude, and behavior. What he wants from you in any given situation may depend on how he feels about his own current level of influence in the company. Take a hard look at whom he influences, and why. Likewise, study the issues he successfully impacts. Accurately reading his positional power will tell you a lot about his state of mind, which in turn will explain a lot of his behavior.

INSIGHTS

Influence

- *Know where he has credibility in the organization.*
- *Learn which leaders he's aligned with (or not).*
- *Recognize what this means for you.*

Your boss's level of influence impacts you.

9 What is his relationship like with his boss?

This is one of the most important insights you can develop about your boss. Like you, he's trying to figure out what his boss prefers and expects. He's trying to look good to his manager, and that has serious implications for you. My advice is to learn everything you can about this relationship—it will explain a lot of his behavior. Is there mutual respect? Does your boss enjoy working for his manager? The reason this impacts you is obvious: if he's not feeling good about this relationship, he's going to be stressed, and you're sure to feel some of that. His relationship with his boss can impact what projects you work on, whether you get promoted, how you're perceived by senior management, even your annual raise or bonus. Frankly, in order for your career to truly take off, you not only need a good relationship with your boss, you need him to have one with his manager, too. That's why you need a lot of insight into this relationship.

For starters, look at how much time they spend together. Does he get face time with his boss? Does he get as much as his peers? Do they have regular one-on-one sessions? Obviously, you're not in all of these meetings, but when you are, pay attention to their interaction style. Does he mostly take orders, or is he advising and influencing decisions? Is he comfortable around his boss? Does he get asked for his opinion? Is he listened to?

I've had lots of experience observing bosses interact with their manager, and the clues to their relationship are right out in the open. For example, Mindy (a mid-level manager in a small company) was essentially afraid of her boss; she believed every meeting could be her last if she wasn't perfect. She'd do anything to please this guy, including misrepresenting data, telling half-truths, even throwing her staff under the bus if necessary. It was painful to be in a meeting with them because it was obvious that Mindy was pandering to his every whim. Her primary motivation was survival. Needless to say, her feedback indicated that her direct reports didn't trust her; there was always a chance she'd cave in and let her boss completely change the scope of the work. The challenge for Mindy was building up her own self-confidence so she could get on a more level playing field with her boss.

Second, listen to how your boss talks about his manager. What signals is he sending about their relationship? Does he drop hints that he's frustrated? Does he share stories that point to alignment issues or stress? Does his body language match his words? You can learn a lot about the relationship with his manager if you read between the lines. Try this exercise: Make a list of the words your boss uses to describe his manager. Check the balance between positive and negative terms and that should tell you all you need to know about how he views the relationship.

In addition to noticing the quantity and quality of interaction, pay attention to the work flow. Where does your boss have carte blanche, and where does he have to check with his manager? What's his level of authority? How closely is his boss managing him? Is he generating most of his own ideas, or does the work emanate from his manager's objectives? What you're looking for here is whether he's controlling his own workload, or just carrying out whatever his boss delegates.

Finally, I'd urge you to establish a direct relationship with your boss's manager. Ask him if he's willing to meet for lunch a few times a year, or give you feedback on selected projects. Arrange to shadow him for a day, or ask to attend internal meetings to observe and learn. Your goal is to establish your own identity with your boss's boss. This is good advice for anyone actually, but it's especially important if your boss has a weak relationship with his manager. Your brand needs to shine through to the big boss, and sometimes the only way to do that is to showcase your ideas and talent directly. William is implementing this strategy. His boss doesn't have a great relationship with his own manager, and William knows his reputation could suffer by association. William developed a strategy for spending time with this senior executive, and he started by asking permission from his boss to approach his manager. When William met with the big boss, he pitched a joint mentoring relationship (he would teach the manager to use the latest technology devices, and the boss would take him on sales calls to strengthen his client skills). The executive agreed and William was able to create his own relationship with this important sponsor.

In my own career, the relationship between my boss and his manager was often my best view into his motives. As I developed insight into how they interacted and felt about each other, I was able to better understand his behavior. Once you feel you've figured out this relationship, verify your impressions with others who work for your boss. Check to see if you're on the right track, then use this insight to adapt to his moods, behavior, and attitude.

INSIGHTS

Boss Relationship

- *Study the relationship between your boss and his boss.*
- *Know that he's as concerned about his boss as you are about him.*
- *Develop a relationship with his boss.*

This relationship greatly influences what your boss wants from you.

⑩ What is his primary motivation?

Now we come to the most important epiphany of all—the insight into your boss's single biggest driver of behavior. In my experience, there is one fundamental motive that steers a boss's actions. I call it "primary motivation." If you had to pick just one motive that accounts for your boss's behavior, how would you describe it? There are a number of common boss motives: job security, advancement, money, recognition, risk aversion, results orientation, complete control (ego), and a desire to be liked by everyone. Do any of these motives explain your boss's behavior? Let's take a look at each of these in more depth.

Your boss may be motivated by job security (fear of losing his job). He may do anything to hang on to his position—every action and decision is made with an eye toward "not rocking the boat." Maybe he's primarily motivated by getting ahead in the organization; all of his behaviors can be traced to his desire to get promoted or look good to senior management. It's possible he is driven by wealth creation; everything he does is about the rewards—getting the highest rating or bonus possible. Perhaps he's motivated by praise and recognition; in that case, he's constantly posturing to be noticed by senior leaders. Maybe he's so risk averse that he'll never make a bold move; his approach is all about not making mistakes or attracting attention. It's possible that he's motivated by perfection; he'll do anything to get specific results that meet his exacting standards. Maybe he has a need to be right or in complete control at all times (high ego, with a micro-managing style). Finally, he may be driven by a need to be liked by everyone, so he avoids conflict at all costs. Your boss may be motivated by one of these typical drivers, or he may have a more specific motive that underlies his behavior.

Whatever it is, your job is to figure it out so you can use that insight to make adjustments in your working relationship.

I believe we all have a primary motivation, that everything we do can be traced back to this fundamental belief, need, or value. As a coach, I've heard just about every possible boss motive story. Jennifer has a boss so focused on himself that he doesn't care about her at all; he doesn't know anything about her life outside of work. Prasad has a boss with an enormous ego—he has to be right about everything, and has to win every debate. Cindy has a boss who avoids risks; hence, nothing gets done because he's afraid to make a controversial move. Lest you think it's all negative, many clients have bosses with positive motives. These managers just want to do good work and help their people grow and develop. They're motivated by achieving results the right way, and by coaching and supporting their teams.

Teri's Epiphany

When I began working with Teri, she'd just been hired as VP of Marketing. While she was being recruited, her boss (the SVP of Marketing) promised her full access to the CEO. However, she soon realized she was never going to present to the CEO; everything had to go through her boss, who personally delivered all of the marketing presentations. After three months, Teri still hadn't met the CEO. Teri shared this revelation with me in one of our sessions: "I've figured out what my boss wants from me—he wants me to be brilliant, but invisible." Teri realized her boss was driven by his own ego and insecurity; he was worried about his standing with the CEO. He wanted the team to do great work, but he was going to take the credit and wasn't about to share the spotlight. Because this wasn't likely to change, Teri and I created a plan for her to build a strong network across the organization, volunteering for cross-company assignments wherever possible. In this way, she was able to establish her own brand, gain a reputation in other departments, and even meet members of the senior team. Eventually, one of these committees presented to the CEO, and the project got the green light. Teri ended up working closely with the CEO on the marketing plan. Instead of getting frustrated with her situation, Teri put her brand to work and paved an alternate path to what she wanted.

What's all this got to do with what your boss wants from you? In a word, everything. Essentially, he wants you to behave in accordance with his primary motivation. He wants you to fall in line with his fundamental motive. If he's insecure about his position, he wants you to keep your head down, too. If he's motivated by advancement, he expects you to make him look good at every turn. If he's driven by rewards or recognition, he may want you to cut corners to get the results that make him a star. If he's a control freak, he wants you to do things his way (and not complain about it). I've always found this single motive to be the most powerful indicator of your boss's behavior. Primary motivation defines what he is all about, and in turn reveals what he really wants from you. Give this question a lot of thought, and see if you can describe the single driving force that accounts for his outlook or behaviors.

Studying your boss is the first step to creating an action plan for improving the relationship. The reflective process starts with knowledge, and I hope these 10 questions have produced some new insights for you. Now, let's turn our attention to a different way of looking at your relationship—what your boss thinks of you.

INSIGHTS

Primary Motivation

- *Figure out the underlying motives driving his behavior.*
- *Validate your analysis with a trusted peer.*
- *Continue to confirm by matching motives to future behaviors.*

This is the biggest single driver of what your boss wants from you.

STEP 2

Consider How Your Boss Sees You

One of the best ways to determine what your boss really wants from you is to look at the relationship from the boss's point of view. That's right, in this section you're going to study the relationship from her perspective. By analyzing yourself through her eyes, you complete the cycle of assessment that started with a study of her motives. This isn't an easy task, by the way; you'll need to look objectively at your skills, experience, and attitude. You'll have to put away your ego or biases to build an impartial view of how she really sees you.

As we take a look at each of these questions in depth, put yourself in your boss's shoes and be as honest as you can about her perception of you. Does she feel you're a star, or merely an average performer? Does she see you as supportive, or are you a pain in the neck? How does she compare you to her other direct reports? Does she believe you have only minor development opportunities or major skill gaps? Does she hold a grudge based on your history together, or is she capable of wiping the slate clean and viewing you objectively? Again, write down your thoughts or observations regarding each question, and carefully consider her likely point of view. By the way, with these questions, you absolutely should gather feedback from peers—they probably have a pretty good idea of how she sees you (chances are she's told them or at least sent clear signals). By honestly considering these questions, you'll complete the picture of what your boss really wants from you. Here are the questions:

How Does Your Boss See You?

Skills

11. What does she value about you?

Strategic Fit

12. How vital are you to her mission?

Development

13. What does she think you need to improve?

Sponsorship

14. How does she represent you to others?

Work History

15. What is her history with you?

⓫ What does she value about you?

I'm going to assume you're a talented professional with a good blend of skills, experience, and ideas. In short, you've got what it takes to succeed at this level, and probably the next. But, does your boss see it that way? How does she view your full set of capabilities? Does she want more from you, or does she actually want less? What does she value most about you, and what does she not appreciate?

Try this exercise: Make a list of your strengths. What are you good at? What skills stand out? Next, place a check mark next to those strengths that fit the role you're in now (some of your talents might not be needed in your current job). Now, move any of these strengths to another list if it's something your boss truly values and leverages. How different are the two lists? I do this exercise with clients and they generally list 10–12 capabilities, most of which fit their current role. But when they select the talents they believe their boss values, the list shrinks to four to six capabilities. This second list doesn't begin to represent the full contribution these people could be making to the business. Is this true for you, too?

The fact is you have many skills, experiences, and ideas that your boss may be ignoring. A common complaint is: *My boss doesn't want to hear about previous work experiences; it's like I never learned anything in my past jobs.* All of us have certain strengths the boss values more than others; your task is to figure out which ones she values, and which ones she doesn't appreciate or utilize.

Why is this insight important? Because what your boss really wants from you is generally what she values most. Think about that. She may view your contribution through a very narrow lens, and actually wants you to maintain that level of impact. That's why you need this reverse perspective. What does she really value? I can remember being thoroughly frustrated by a boss who refused to consider my ideas about a new way of conducting performance reviews. I had experience with another company that she just wouldn't listen to, and it was driving me crazy. Eventually, I realized she had placed my skills and expertise in one compartment, and wasn't going to use my ideas to solve problems in another one. In a sense, she wanted about 65% of my capability, not 100%. Was this discouraging? You bet. Was it better to have this epiphany than not? Most definitely.

Let's say you've had a lot of experience with new product design, but she doesn't want that from you; instead, she wants sales execution. You'd like to leverage a strength, while she wants the exact opposite from you. Maybe you have some great ideas about process improvement, but she never asks for them. Perhaps you're good at leading teams, but she's got you in an individual contributor role because she doesn't value your people-management skills. Maybe you could build a whole new service offering, but she doesn't want more work to manage (remember, her true motives may result in some very counterintuitive behavior).

Most of the people I work with find this insight to be both painful and useful. The simple act of looking at your own capabilities through your boss's eyes can explain a lot about what she wants from you. In some cases, she wants you in a box where you deliver specific results and nothing more, or she wants to use certain skills from your toolbox, but not all of them. Sometimes that's because those skills aren't called for in your role; other times, it's because she doesn't want (or know how) to expand your contribution.

Doug is experiencing this frustration with his boss. He's

really good at financial planning and analysis, and would love to help with the team's budget (which he did in two previous roles). However, the boss doesn't value Doug's financial skills (for whatever reason) and regularly turns down his requests to get involved with the budget process. This fits my experience with certain bosses; they like to have everyone on the team playing a very specific role, which comes from a desire to maintain complete control. In these cases, additional skills aren't recognized because they don't fit the model of how the boss wants to run the team.

In other cases, your boss may recognize your talent, but doesn't want to use it. This is especially true of the insecure boss, the one who is afraid you're actually more talented than she is. Let's say your boss knows you're good at building relationships, but doesn't give you credit for it. It may be that she isn't good at this herself, so she's not going to recognize your talents in this area. Here's another example: your boss knows you're good at creating innovative ideas to improve the business, but she likes things the way they are, so she's not going to leverage your creative skills. Or this common scenario, where she understands you're well connected outside the company, but envies your network and professional status; therefore, you're probably not going to get credit for this or be allowed to fully leverage your connections.

I know this can be frustrating; nothing's worse than having a boss who doesn't recognize or utilize your true talents. But this is a real situation, and you need to be fully aware of the consequences. If you're not sure what she wants from you, it might be because you're not seeing your skill set from her perspective. In my experience, a lot of bosses want less from you, not more.

The Unrecognized Talent

Olivia was a VP in charge of new product development. She was considered highly creative by her peers, who regularly asked for her input on projects. However, even though her boss respected the way Olivia ran new products, he never sought her input on other creative challenges. When the time came to plan the annual sales conference, Olivia's peers lobbied the boss to put her in charge of the event because they knew she'd take it in a new, creative direction. Olivia even asked her boss directly for the project, but he turned her down; he didn't think she had enough of a "feel for the event." Later, Olivia told me: "I don't think he wants me anywhere near this—he's afraid I'll do something drastically different. I don't think he wants to take the risk." The boss was definitely not valuing Olivia's primary strength, and her storyline became, *He doesn't appreciate my creative talent*. I could tell this was upsetting her, so we created a strategy for her to take another run at the assignment. Before asking for the task again, she reviewed the content and flow of past conferences, and developed a proposal that would incorporate a few of her creative ideas, but not alter the format dramatically. She also assured him she'd partner with the head of Sales before finalizing the plan. Her persistence paid off and the boss gave her the project. By recognizing (but ultimately not accepting) the boss's view of her skills, she made a few alterations to her approach that allowed her to demonstrate her true talent.

So, which skills does your boss appreciate? What is she leveraging? What is she ignoring? You need to take an inventory, understand the implications, and act to expand her view of how you can add more value.

Try this: Pick out a skill your boss isn't leveraging, and look for ways to demonstrate your capability. Partner with a peer on a project outside your normal scope of work, or bring the boss a proposal for something you can do in your spare time. Speak up in meetings about certain topics to establish your knowledge and credibility. Tell stories in your one-on-ones about talents you've applied in the past that fit current challenges. In other words, take responsibility for how your boss sees you. Don't let her dictate how the organization views your skill set. Make small but steady strides to expand her view of what you can offer. The more she sees you as a well-rounded asset, the more she'll start using you in different ways. If you can change her perception of your capabilities, you may change what she wants from you.

INSIGHTS

Skills & Capabilities

- *Figure out which of your skills and capabilities she values.*
- *Understand what she doesn't recognize or value.*
- *Act to expand her view of your talents.*

Know what your boss values about you.

⓬ How vital are you to her mission?

When you studied your boss in Step 1, you captured her priorities and agenda to understand her focus areas. Let's go back to that concept—how important are you to her overall mission? Of all the things she's trying to deliver, how critical are you, really? In relation to all the projects in her group, where do you stand in the "pecking order" of deliverables? It shouldn't come as a surprise that your boss has different priorities. While you may think your project is critically important, can you be sure she feels the same way? Is your work in the top tier of urgent concerns? What about you personally? Are you thought of as one of the vital resources she needs to carry out the mission?

David found out the hard way that he wasn't front and center on his boss's radar screen. He was hired specifically to launch the new corporate university, and his boss assured him this was her top priority. However, as David got into the project and needed her help, she was noncommittal or worse—completely unavailable. David was confused. Hadn't she told him this was at the top of her list? What David failed to recognize was that a couple of other fires had flared up, and his boss was focused on putting them out. As a result, David lost valuable momentum because he had counted on his boss's active involvement; he hadn't built a business case strong enough to move the launch forward without her sponsorship.

Sometimes it's more than a mere shift in priorities. Do you recognize the major themes of your boss's mission? Do you see where she's taking the department, and are you part of these plans? Do your skills, experience, and attitude fit her agenda? A good example of this is when your boss decides to outsource certain work, or plans a reduction in force in her group. In this case, she's playing the long game; she's focused on radically changing everything about her department, and may even have her own exit strategy planned for when the task is completed. Do you really think your new project is going to compete with this more strategic, overarching objective? No way. Your boss knows more about what's going on across the enterprise than you do. She sees and hears things you don't, and won't always discuss them with you. As a result, she may be shifting priorities or pointing the department in a new direction without telling you, which means your value is being evaluated continuously.

Do you know how important you are (personally) to her mission? Combine the previous insight about what she values most about you with her agenda, and you'll have an answer to this question. How indispensable are you? In today's world, no one is completely safe in any job. What are the latest clues about your skills-mission match? Has anything happened recently to change your value as a direct report? Like you, I've seen several colleagues who got left behind because their capabilities didn't match the current mission. They didn't recognize that the value equation was changing, and acted too late to do anything about it.

I don't ask this question to add stress or cause you to worry about your place on the team. I just want you to assess your value to the boss's mission, from her perspective. Take a hard look at your contribution and what you're working on. Are you still important to the mission? Is that mission evolving? Does she see you as an important (and necessary) part of the future? Be objective about your value; chances are you're overestimating it. Don't assume because you were solid with your boss six months ago that you're still seen as a must-have part of her team. The business may have changed, or your group may have lost or gained stature in the organization. I've experienced this in my own career. I worked for a company that started making acquisitions into an adjacent business, one with a much lower profit margin. As a result, our entire cost model needed to change. We had built a high-touch employee model; now we were being asked to move to an employee self-serve format. Those of us who adapted to this change in mission thrived; those who didn't had a difficult time adjusting. Not surprisingly, the boss valued those who were on board with the new model.

If you judge your value correctly, it should provide some useful insights. For one thing, it may calm you down and keep you from annoying her if she's focused temporarily elsewhere. More importantly, you might recognize a broader change in the overall mission in time to make a few adjustments to your game. Analyze what your boss is focused on, and how involved you are in those priorities. Look at your full range of capabilities and evaluate how they fit with her agenda. Then, adapt your behavior, attitude, and contribution to the mission. In other words, give your boss a reason to see you as part of the future, not the past.

INSIGHTS

Importance to the Mission

- *Know her agenda and the overall mission.*
- *Evaluate how you fit into the mission.*
- *Make the necessary adjustments in your attitude or behavior.*

Stay relevant to your boss's agenda.

⓭ What does she think you need to improve?

Have you ever considered that your boss doesn't think you're perfect? That you're not finished developing? It's a safe bet she feels your skills could use a little polish. Since we all have development opportunities, what does she want you to work on? Has she told you? Even if she has, do you really believe that's all she feels you need to improve?

This question can't be answered by looking at your performance appraisal or development plan. Sure, you both agreed upon some growth areas in your most recent review, and those may be legitimate development opportunities. But what else does she want you to work on? Think about her motives and preferences. Is there anything she's not telling you because it reveals too much about what she wants from you?

Kevin is in this situation. At his mid-year review, Kevin's boss suggested he work on his coaching and delegation skills (Kevin agreed these were opportunities). However, he also suspects the boss wants him to work on listening and taking direction more effectively. Why? Because whenever Kevin doesn't follow his boss's specific direction, she gets upset. She wants Kevin to do exactly what she tells him to do, and whenever Kevin follows his own path, he feels the boss's wrath. Why doesn't Kevin's boss just come out and tell him to improve these skills? Because she knows it will sound silly; the only examples she can give Kevin are times when he's not done precisely what she wanted. She's savvy enough to know it looks petty to suggest a development need that really isn't there. Still, if Kevin is right, how long should he ignore this unspoken development suggestion? My recommendation was to start demonstrating deeper listening behaviors now, to get ahead of what may well become a career-derailer if the boss's perceptions don't change (after all, Kevin can always use improved listening skills). The idea is to infer what your boss wants you to improve, even if she's not telling you directly.

Here's another example. Sara's boss summed up her development opportunities in a simple statement: "You just need to be more like me." The boss thought she was providing a pretty clear development roadmap, but it only served to frustrate Sara. Not only was the feedback broad and opaque, it was arrogant and condescending. The message was: *"You're doing it wrong; just copy my style and behaviors."* In this case, Sara didn't have to guess what her boss wanted her to improve because the blueprint was right in front of her. In the end, Sara chose not to adopt her boss's exact style; instead, we worked on specific leadership skills based on feedback from her peers and direct reports. However, Sara certainly received a clear message about what her boss wanted from her, and that insight proved valuable in itself.

A Missed Development Signal

Bill was one of my most capable clients, a recognized thought leader in his field. When I met Bill, he was irritated by his boss's formal meeting style and rigorous approach to decision making. Bill preferred casual discussions he called "thinking out loud." When he would meet with his boss, Bill was argumentative and resistant to her iterative process and desire for data. Stubbornly, Bill kept trying to guide the boss to decisions based on anecdotal evidence, and it wasn't working. Not only was he getting frustrated, he was pushing all the wrong buttons with his boss. At the same time, the boss wasn't providing direct feedback about this disconnect; she wasn't being clear that Bill needed to develop a more rigorous style. Through several coaching conversations, Bill came to understand he wasn't going to change his boss; deliberate analysis and multiple review meetings were just how she did things. When he began to change his *own* style, their relationship improved dramatically. Bill did two things that allowed him to have more influence: First, he upped his game in terms of gathering data to support his assertions. Every recommendation now came with solid evidence. Second, he started preparing multiple options, so his boss could be part of the decision making process. By understanding what his boss wanted him to improve, Bill set aside his own ego, changed his approach, and started getting the result he wanted all along—to be recognized as the expert.

This insight—what your boss really wants to you work on—is an important piece of the relationship puzzle. In your next development discussion, listen carefully to her suggestions, but also listen to what she's not saying. If you suspect she wants you to improve some aspect of your skills or style, ask her directly. A great question is: *What can I work on that would improve our relationship?* Another is: *What skills can I develop that would add more value for you?* Your job is to take the guesswork out of what she wants you to improve. By sharpening your insight into her motives and preferences, you should be able to deduce what she wants you to develop. Then, ask for specific feedback about those skills or behaviors, and you'll create a clear picture (once and for all) about what she wants from you—at least as it pertains to your development plan. Ultimately, you may choose to not work on those areas, but at least you'll drive the discussion and the resulting insights out into the open.

INSIGHTS

Development Opportunities

- *Figure out what skills and behaviors she wants you to improve.*
- *Work backward from her motives and preferences.*
- *Ask her directly about development you suspect she wants to see.*

Be clear about what your boss wants you to work on.

⓮ How does she represent you to others?

One of your boss's responsibilities involves evaluating your performance and potential. In doing so, she will be sharing this assessment with other leaders in the company. If you work in a large firm, this happens in the formal talent review process, where senior leaders gather to discuss you and your peers. If you're in a smaller company, it's more informal, but she's still sharing her evaluation of you with her boss and others. So, do you have an idea of how she's representing you? How she's describing your performance, attitude, and work ethic? Whether she supports your potential to advance in the company? This might be the hardest of all insights to read and verify, but it's important that you have some idea of how she's presenting you to the organization. There are at least three evaluations she's making at all times, and each has to do with what she wants from you.

First, she's comparing you to a standard or model of what she expects from a direct report. If she has been managing people for a while, she has a strong sense of what she wants in an employee (remember her preferences). Try this exercise: Write down the qualities of her ideal employee and compare yourself to this list. How well do you match up? This is the first test of whether you're delivering what she wants, and most of this is likely to be about your makeup. Do you match her ideal profile of work ethic, attitude, passion, teamwork, etc.? While this may seem like a comparison to a fixed standard, it's more than that. Fair or not, your boss is talking to other managers about how you match her perfect-employee model. In fact, there may be cultural norms that make this prototype fairly common across the organization.

Second, it's a fact of life that she is comparing you to your peers. Officially this is discouraged, but trust me, it happens all the time. In conversations with her boss or other leaders (either formal or informal), she is ranking her direct reports along a number of dimensions. Do you know your place in this pecking order? Do you know how she discusses this list with her peers, and how she's representing you specifically? Do you know which of your colleagues are giving her exactly what she wants, and why? If your boss has ever said, *You need to be more like John or Susan*, then you can be sure she is comparing you to your peers. While this is totally inappropriate, you won't get a clearer picture of what she wants from you! I get this complaint all the time from clients. Yolanda had a boss spend their entire performance appraisal meeting comparing her to her peers. Besides being incredibly uncomfortable, this only confused and infuriated Yolanda; she didn't know what to do with this bizarre feedback.

While the peer comparison may be unseemly, it's one way that senior leaders discuss and score your contribution. Are you better than John? Are you more or less valuable than Susan? Here's an awkward exercise you might try (write it down, then destroy the list after you're done). From your boss's perspective, rank her direct reports from "favorite" to "least favorite." Where are you on the list? More importantly, what are the people above you doing that you're not doing? Now, write out their behaviors, and compare those to your own. Are there any adjustments you're willing to make in your approach? When I ask people to do this exercise, it always results in powerful insights about what the boss wants. In fact, some can pinpoint exactly what John or Susan are doing that works well with the boss, which unlocks the insights they need to plot a course of action. In this case, the clues to what she wants are literally all around you—all you have to do is pay attention to her relationships with your peers.

Finally, when she represents you to the organization, she's

comparing you to people in other departments. Do you know what these comparisons are like? Think back to the people she respects in the company; how do you stack up? Are these fair comparisons, and are these people worth emulating? If at all possible, try to find out the details of how she represented you in these meetings. The only way to really know is to ask her directly and hope she tells the truth. In my experience, if she says: *I told them you're doing fine*, she's not giving you the full story. On the other hand, if she provides details about the conversation, what others leaders said, the discussion of your development needs, etc., she's probably giving you an accurate picture of how she represented you. Mostly, this will be a "feel" type of insight based on experience and intuition. The given is that she's talking about you; the wild card is what she's actually saying. Try to imagine how this conversation would go. What positives is she highlighting, and what is she mentioning that isn't so positive?

In my corporate life, I led the talent review process for four large companies, and the conversation goes like this: *Here's what Nick is doing well, and here's what he needs to work on.* I learned to read between the lines on the second half of the discussion; many times, it wasn't a real development need at all, but something that didn't fit the boss's preferences. Is this happening to you? As best you can, try to determine how she's representing you. After all, this is the primary way senior leaders get a sense of your capabilities, and you need to know how your brand is being portrayed across the company. There may be nothing you can do to control what she says, but you can certainly do something with the knowledge of what she's saying.

INSIGHTS

Representing You

- *Know your boss's model of the perfect employee.*
- *Be aware of how she compares you to your peers.*
- *Learn how your boss represents you to the organization.*

Know how your boss is talking about you.

⓯ What is her history with you?

The final question to consider from your boss's perspective has to do with your complete history of working with her. Has her opinion of you evolved over time? Has the relationship improved lately, or is it in steady decline? If it's the latter, can you point to a specific incident that caused the relationship to go off the rails? Your track record with your boss provides a number of insights that can be quite revealing, especially taken in context with all you've learned thus far about her motives and views of you. Let's look at three historical dynamics in particular: 1) how the relationship started, 2) how it evolved, and 3) where it is now.

Let's start with how you got together in the first place. Did she hire you? Did she join the team after you? Was she a peer who became your boss? Each of these scenarios has different implications for what she wants from you. If she hired you, she probably believes she was clear about what she wanted from you. Think back to those conversations. Did you get a clear sense of mission, and if so, have you strayed from it? You may have forgotten this, but chances are she hasn't. In the interviews, did you trust your instincts about her or ignore them? Were there signs even then that you overlooked just to get the job? If so, you can't really fault her consistency—she sent signals about what kind of boss she would be (this isn't particularly helpful now, but it's a good lesson for next time).

If you were already on the team when she joined, how was her assimilation? What clues did you pick up during her first few weeks, and what did you do with them? Did you try to bend her to your will, or did you quickly adapt to her style? Again, she probably remembers her entry onto the team better than you do and her opinion of you probably includes those critical first interactions. What insights can you draw from looking at this from her perspective?

Finally, if she was a peer who became your boss, we're talking about the most challenging transition of all. Entire books have been written on this subject, and it's safe to assume this move was filled with drama. From her perspective, did you make it easy for her, or did you fight it? Were you supportive from the beginning, or did you hold back your full commitment? Put yourself in her shoes, and consider the history. Can you see how this would color her views of you, even today? These early-days insights can be illuminating, but you need to see them through her eyes to really understand the full story.

Next, consider how the relationship has evolved. Since you first met, has the relationship been consistent, or are you on a roller-coaster ride? Try this exercise: Draw a horizontal line across the middle of a piece of paper. Working from left to right, record the general date and description of any critical episodes that impacted your relationship. Positive events go above the line; negative incidents go below. The challenge is to do this from her perspective. How would she characterize these experiences? Are you looking at these incidents the same way? Did you consider her perspective at the time, and how she would remember the event? Some bosses forgive and forget, but many don't. You may be missing what she has filed away over the years about your behavior or attitude. She might remember those seemingly innocent disagreements very differently.

The evolution of your relationship says a lot about its current state. Can you pinpoint the exact event where things started to change between you and your boss? By considering the incident from her point of view, can you see its impact more clearly? If so, is there anything you can do about it now? If it's in the recent past, perhaps you can bring it up for discussion, acknowledge its impact, apologize, etc. Jonathan had this type of insight when we did the timeline exercise. He realized that when he had gone over his boss's head with a budget request three months earlier, their relationship had taken a turn for the worse. We quickly planned an approach for Jonathan to discuss this with his boss in an attempt to clear the air, which he was able to do. However, until he saw the event from her perspective, Jonathan never appreciated the full extent of the damage he'd done to the relationship.

Still Paying the Price

The first thing Jeffrey told me when we started working together was that he and his boss "have a history." Apparently, the relationship had been fine at first, but had soured over a single, contentious issue involving one of Jeffrey's direct reports. This employee had made an error in a transaction with a vendor, costing the company a lot of money. The boss wanted Jeffrey to fire this employee immediately. Jeffrey refused. In the end, Jeffrey was not *made* to fire the employee, and she stayed on. Jeffrey still doesn't know why his boss didn't play the "I'm making you" card, but in some ways, he's suffering a fate worse than if he'd been forced to choose between his job and his principles. The boss has been cold and distant ever since; she doesn't ask Jeffrey for input in meetings, holds back assignments, and doesn't interact with Jeffrey's people. She's freezing him out, and Jeffrey believes it's a ploy to get him to quit. By helping Jeffrey see things from the boss's perspective, we decided to try the direct approach. Jeffrey asked his boss for a meeting in which he told her what he had learned from the experience, and how he wanted to put the episode behind them. He didn't admit he should have fired the employee, but he did acknowledge that he should have listened better to her point of view. As it turned out, this approach worked; the relationship improved. They will both always remember it, of course, but the agreement to move past it seems to be holding.

This brings us to the here and now. If you could somehow get inside your boss's head, how would she describe the relationship? Don't get caught up in how you'd describe it; instead, consider this question from her perspective. What does she get from you? Can she count on you and do you have her back? Are you a team player? Are you high maintenance? Does she look forward to meeting with you?

The bottom line is this: You're not the only one in this relationship. Your boss has a perception of you, and it's just as legitimate as the one you have of her. You may not agree with her view, but you can't deny her the right to have one. Furthermore, your boss is human, which means she has a long memory. Everything about your work history gets wrapped up in her current perception of you. Don't count on your boss being the "live and let live" type; chances are she's not forgotten anything that happened in the past. Draw the important insights from your shared history, and you'll understand even more about what she wants from you.

Looking at the relationship from your boss's perspective is an important step in the reflective process, and I hope you gained a new level of awareness from these questions. Now, let's move to the final step—creating an action plan for adapting your own attitude and behavior to make the relationship work more effectively.

INSIGHTS

Your Shared History

- *Consider how your boss sees your full history together.*
- *Be aware of how specific events impact your relationship.*
- *Know how she would describe the relationship right now.*

Assess the full history of your relationship.

STEP 3

Take Responsibility for the Relationship

Sections 1 and 2 were all about awareness and understanding. The questions were designed to open your mind by taking a deeper look at your boss's motives, and by seeing the relationship from his or her perspective. Equipped with these insights, it's time for you to take responsibility for the relationship. Remember, you're not going to change your boss; improvement will come by modifying your attitude and behavior. In this section, I'll provide general tips and techniques for making these adjustments, and offer specific recommendations for four common boss/motive scenarios.

It Starts with Attitude

Let's start by discussing the most important adjustment you need to make—your attitude. Any progress you make with your boss has to be rooted in a new way of looking at him. You'll never successfully change your behavior if you don't first adjust your attitude. I believe these two concepts are equally important; you need to be intentional about changing your attitude *and* your behavior. Adjusting your attitude starts with changing the way you view your boss.

One client's story illustrates why attitude is so important. A few years ago, Paul was asked by his boss to work on his listening skills. Paul put all of the classic listening behaviors in place: removing distractions, better eye contact and body language, asking lots of questions, etc. For a while, he made good progress, but I later learned Paul had regressed; he'd gone back to being a lousy listener. Why? He never changed his attitude about listening to the boss. Paul never bought into the feedback, and secretly maintained a mindset of, *I'm smarter than he is so why should I listen to him?* Needless to say, the boss was unimpressed with Paul's development progress. Paul's new behaviors didn't stick because they weren't anchored in a new attitude, a mindset that could be summed up as, *I need to become a better listener; this is important to my boss.* As a coach, I've seen this happen a few times; some clients believe all they have to do is adjust their behavior, but they don't commit to changing their attitude toward the boss relationship. This doesn't work. Your heart won't be in it, and the boss will see right through it. That's why it's so important to identify and actually make an attitude adjustment; your mindset serves as the mental foundation for your behavior. Look at it this way, if you can change the way you think about the relationship, anything's possible from a behavior standpoint, and you'll have a much better chance of maintaining success.

Defining Attitude

What do I mean by attitude? The dictionary defines attitude as a feeling or emotion toward a fact or state. That works nicely—

your attitude toward your boss is definitely emotional, and is tied to the changing state of the relationship. So let's agree that by attitude we mean feelings or emotions. What's more, your attitude can be seen, heard, and felt by others—body language, tone of voice, and facial expressions are the physical manifestation of your emotions. Let's face it; you're not hiding your attitude from your boss. He can pick up on your attitude just by looking at you (by the way, so can everyone else).

The first thing you have to do is articulate your current attitude toward your boss. Talking about this works best, so enlist a trusted colleague to be your peer coach for this exercise (if you're not comfortable with that, at least write it down). Describe or write every emotion, thought, and feeling you have about your boss. Explain why you feel this way, and share or write examples that explain your mindset. There's a lot to digest here; the boss's motives, the history of the relationship, critical interactions, etc. Bring it all to the surface. In order to adjust your attitude, you first have to define it. You have a specific attitude toward your boss, and if you're going to successfully change the relationship, you need to determine where you can make modifications to this current mindset.

Modify Your Story

So how do you do it? How do you change your attitude toward the boss? It's not as hard as you think, but it does require an open mind, a new sense of maturity, and a commitment to seek the truth. There are three things you need to do: 1) gain a new perspective on the relationship, 2) modify your story, and 3) communicate your new attitude. The good news is you've already done the first step. In order to create a new mindset about your boss, you have to see her in a different light. This is why you studied her motives and looked at yourself through her eyes; you need these insights to take the next step.

The second step involves modifying your story. That's right, you're living in a story, a story you created. It's the story of you and your boss from a single perspective—yours. It might be a story of persecution, betrayal, or lost trust. Maybe it's a story of missed opportunity, or of being held back. Regardless of the narrative, the story is one-sided; you've cast yourself as the hero, and your boss as the villain. You've convinced yourself that you're right, and she's wrong.

Your story is very powerful; you've told it to yourself (and others) so often it's become reality. But it's a distorted reality that you've invented and rationalized to justify the relationship. Even if much of the story is true, in your mind you've probably pushed it beyond the limits of credibility. Don't believe me? Next time you talk about your boss to a colleague, spouse, or friend, listen to what you're saying. Doesn't it sound like you're the victim here? Trust me, I've heard some pretty tragic boss stories over the years (and told some myself, too).

However, there are two sides to every story. Regardless of how you feel about your boss, she feels differently about you. However you tell the story, she would share a different version. The second step in adjusting your attitude is recognizing this and crafting the most objective description possible of your relationship with your boss. In other words, you need to modify the story. Examples of this include:

Old Story: My boss purposefully withholds information from me.

New Story: I need to ask for more context; he doesn't always share the full picture.

Old Story: My boss isn't interested in my projects; I'm not on his radar screen.
New Story: His focus is elsewhere right now, but I'm still part of his annual goals.

Old Story: My boss doesn't want me to have a relationship with her manager.
New Story: She values alignment and wants to stay closely connected up the chain.

Old Story: My boss is giving away part of my group to punish me.
New Story: She's freeing me up to drive better results in my core areas.

Old Story: My boss doesn't want my ideas.
New Story: He does, but I need to bring practical solutions with more evidence.

Can you feel the attitude adjustment? See how the story changes if you look at it through a broader lens? Modifying your boss story is a necessary part of creating a new mindset. Here's an example that illustrates the power of changing your story. Many years ago, I carried around a story about one of my bosses. We were struggling to get on the same page, and I was convinced he disliked me, didn't trust me, and even wanted to fire me. I was spending my entire weekend worrying about what he thought of me. I was miserable, and was making my wife miserable, too. All I could talk about was my relationship with the boss, and how it was rapidly deteriorating. One day I was telling this to a coworker, and she said something that changed my life: "Steve, you're overanalyzing this. You spend way more time worrying about Mike than he spends worrying about you. He doesn't spend one minute thinking about you outside the office." Wow. My story had included this image of my boss spending his weekends thinking about our relationship, scheming for ways to get me, etc. Her simple observation really opened my eyes and I realized she was right—Mike didn't view the relationship the same way I did. I was living in a story that was completely unfounded, and frankly, I was feeding it, making it worse every week. Are you doing this? Are you creating a story that's literally pulling you down and making the situation worse? How much of it is real, and how much of it are you making up?

Take a hard look at your story, and really strive to understand how you're representing the relationship. As a coach, I'll often record the story and play it back for clients; there's nothing like hearing oneself whine about the boss to realize exactly how it sounds. Again, enlist a peer to help you with this. Start telling your story and have them repeat what they're hearing; the one-sidedness of the story might surprise you. Once you've admitted to yourself the true nature of the story, modify it. Take every element and restate it in the most objective terms possible. Use all your insight and rewrite the script. It's amazing how different the two stories can be; the first is generally a victim tale, while the second is an impartial view of the relationship that takes into account motives and circumstances. When you've modified your story, you'll be ready for the final step: communicating your new attitude to the world.

Communicate Your New Story

Changing your story won't mean a thing if you don't share the new version. Thus, the third step in adjusting your attitude involves taking your new story public. If your peers and boss don't hear a new point of view, you haven't made any real progress. There are two ways to do this. First, you have to literally tell your colleagues a different story. Your peers and direct reports need to hear you talk differently about the boss. They have to feel like you're taking responsibility for the relationship.

Modifying your story involves checking your negativity at the door, and getting out of the victim mode. Stop complaining about your boss—immediately. Replace sarcastic comments with benefit-of-the-doubt statements. Walk away from pity parties with colleagues, or better yet, turn them into productive brainstorming sessions about how to work with the boss more effectively. Be objective when talking about the boss; let others know you're seeing all sides of her perspective.

You get the idea. I can't say it more simply—stop talking about your boss negatively, and start talking about her objectively. You're digging a hole with your current story, and every time you tell it you go deeper and deeper. At some point, your peers will tune you out, or your boss will get wind of the story and you'll do even more damage to the relationship. Trust me, it's not worth it. Are you ready to adjust and improve the relationship, or are you going to stay on a destructive path?

Here's a story that illustrates how important it is to change your story. Lori was complaining non-stop to her peers about not getting promoted. She told everyone about the boss promising her a promotion then withholding it to "keep me in my place." The first thing Lori changed about her attitude was this part of her story: from that moment on, she never once brought up the promotion issue again, to her boss or her peers. The coaching I gave Lori was: "Take this topic out of the equation; don't let it be ammunition for others to use when assessing your attitude or performance." By eliminating the victim mentality from her story, Lori removed the whiner tag that others had naturally ascribed to her.

If you need convincing that this can work, look around you. You know that peer who always keeps his cool, who stays positive and constructive, who's a mature, even-keeled professional? The one who has found a way to peacefully coexist with the boss, despite all the same issues? That's your role model; that's who you want to emulate. That's the brand you're going for with this new attitude. Matt had such a peer. This person would routinely ask Matt: "Why do you let the boss get to you? Can't you see what she wants?" Matt admired how well his colleague had adapted to the boss's style and was intrigued by how he managed the relationship. I encouraged him to learn more: "Matt, there's your blueprint; talk to him and learn how he does it."

I really believe in leaning on a trusted peer to help you with your story, often, they can be your best source of guidance and inspiration. Here's an example that shows the value of peer coaching. Hannah was struggling to align with her boss on strategy and goals. Not an uncommon predicament, right? Here was Hannah's story: *He doesn't understand this field, and is micromanaging the process. He won't listen. He's more worried about what his boss wants than doing what's right. He's inflexible, stubborn, and has to control every detail. He doesn't care about doing this well, all he cares about is making it easy for everyone.* Does that story sound objective? Of course not; Hannah was in full victim mode. By the way, she was peddling this story to anyone who would listen. What attitude do you think she was projecting? Fortunately, a trusted peer suggested she change her story.

As Hannah worked to modify her story, it turned into this: *We're looking at this from two different perspectives, both of which are legitimate. It's not personal; he just has another opinion—one that I need to work harder to influence. I know he's motivated by pleasing his boss, so there may be other circumstances that are causing him to take this stance; perhaps he's negotiating a trade-off between my project and others. Finally, he's got experience with our culture that I need to consider—the company may be unable to absorb this particular process right now.* Sounds different, doesn't it? The story changes if you step back and don't take it so personally. That's really the key to modifying your story—stepping back and removing all the personal baggage. Because you studied your boss, you know the root of his behavior. Craft a new story that incorporates all you've learned. I guarantee it will help improve the relationship.

Look, I'm not asking you to be Pollyanna; you don't have to make a 180 degree turn. Some things are still going to bug you about your boss. The difference is how you're letting those behaviors affect you, and how you're choosing to act or react. Your new story about the boss has to account for his motives. Your perceived attitude has to evolve from being a victim to being in control. From a mindset of, *I can't handle this* to, *I got this.* Let your colleagues hear that story. I guarantee it will change others' perception of you, and you'll become more confident and comfortable the more you tell it.

Change Your Behaviors

The second way you're going to communicate your new story is by changing the way you behave around your boss. Where she's concerned, you can't just talk the talk; you have to show her you've adjusted your attitude. You do this by adopting new behaviors (or stopping unproductive ones). So let's move from attitude to behaviors and talk about visibly taking responsibility for the relationship.

My clients and I have a code phrase for this task. We call it "51 percent." In coaching sessions, I'll regularly ask them: "Are you taking 51 percent?" This is my way of reminding people they have to go more than half-way when it comes to improving the boss relationship. It's not a 50–50 proposition; you have to be more committed to the objective than your boss. Obviously, the 51 percent figure is symbolic; what I want you to take away is that you have to do most of the work in moving this relationship forward.

Visible behavior adjustments come in four types: actions to stop, start, emphasize, or de-emphasize. Some of these changes are subtle, and some are very deliberate. Let's start with behaviors you should stop. Generally, if there is something you're doing that is really irritating your boss, stop it immediately. In fact, most people tell me that stopping a behavior was the most productive adjustment they made as they worked to improve the boss relationship. Examples of typical behaviors that people choose to stop include:

- Drawing him into uncomfortable debates during staff meetings
- Meeting with his peers without his knowledge
- Arguing with her over small presentation/report preferences
- Resisting her desired work schedule
- Pushing a point of view so far that it angers/frustrates him
- Whining or complaining (about anything)

Try this exercise: make a list of any behaviors that annoy your boss. Be honest; you know which of his buttons you're pushing. Think back to his preferences, and how he views you. Now, which of these behaviors could you stop doing immediately? At what cost? I bet some of these behaviors could be dropped right now and you wouldn't lose any access or leverage (actually, you're likely to gain more than you lose). Give careful thought to what he really wants from you. I think you'll find that stopping certain behaviors is more useful than starting new ones. I remember a boss who hated it when I questioned him in public. To adjust, I simply moved those conversations to our one-on-ones, and that simple act improved our relationship.

In other cases, you need to adopt new behaviors. Again, look at your most successful peers—what are they doing that you can copy? Hudson had a boss that nearly everyone struggled with—except one of his peers. I asked Hudson what this person did differently, and he rattled off about five things his peer did that seemed to work with the boss. My obvious question was: "What's keeping you from doing some of these things?" Hudson decided to adopt two of the behaviors: 1) giving the boss more lead time to review materials, and 2) creating and sending an agenda in advance of their one-on-one meetings. Both of these required a little extra work, which he'd been unwilling to do. However, by observing the actions of a peer, Hudson added a few new behaviors to his game and met the boss's expectations more successfully. So, what new behaviors do you need to adapt? Where do you need to change your approach? What do you need to start doing differently?

I'll share one of my behavior adjustments, and while this change isn't possible for everyone, it paid off for me. I once had a boss who valued an early start to the day; if she didn't see you early in the morning, she didn't think you were working hard (it didn't matter how late you stayed—any work you did after she went home didn't count). I generally arrived around 8:30 a.m., which didn't fit her style at all. When I shifted my work schedule to arrive at 7:00 a.m., our relationship improved immediately. Now, I was able to make that adjustment in my schedule, and I understand not everyone has that flexibility. But it illustrates my point that when it comes to behavior starts, look at her preferences for clues. Determine the raw spots in your relationship, and you'll find things to start doing that will make those go away. Here are some examples of common behavior starts:

- Talking positively about her to your peers
- Introducing her to influential people (inside or outside the company)
- Volunteering for a difficult assignment
- Providing more relevant background or data than requested
- Using the word "opportunity" instead of "problem"
- Providing her with organizational context she's not getting elsewhere

Other times, all you have to do is dial something up or down. In these cases, I coach people to examine what they could "do more" and "do less." The behavior is all right, they're just overdoing it (or vice versa). Brett needed to do this when it came to checking in with his boss; he was simply doing it too often. He was worried about making a mistake, which ironically, made his boss doubt him more. Brett had to de-emphasize this behavior, and fast. So, what behaviors could you do more or less often? Think about frequency and intensity when you plan these adjustments. Here are some examples of common "more and less" behavior changes:

- Always remembering to give him a heads-up on sensitive issues
- Asking for his perspective more often on your tougher decisions
- Always bringing more than one possible solution to the discussion
- Modulating your speaking frequency and duration in staff meetings

- Making fewer drop-in interruptions by his office
- Disagreeing publicly (do it in private)

Changing just a few behaviors can bring you back into alignment with your boss. It can make the difference between delivering what he wants and missing the mark. Remember, you are the only one who can control your own behavior; you just have to have the discipline and commitment to make the right adjustments.

Write a Development Plan

Adopting (and sticking with) new behaviors has the effect of feeding your new attitude. In fact, the attitude-behavior connection is so critical that I recommend documenting both adjustments in a formal development plan (see *Figure 1*). In the left column, capture the two or three areas of the boss relationship you want to focus on. In the middle column, write the attitude or mindset adjustments you're committed to making—your new story. In the far right column, write any new behaviors you will start, stop, or fine-tune; actions that your peers and boss will actually notice. These final two columns work together. Attitude declarations align with new behaviors. I think you'll find that both adjustments are necessary if you're going to truly improve your relationship with the boss.

I really believe you'll make more progress if your ideas are written as a formal development plan. The act of writing a plan serves to cement your intentions. So write it out, keep the plan with you, and refer to it often. Update it as you experience progress with your boss. If you feel comfortable doing so, share it with a trusted peer and ask them to coach you. Ask: *What are you*

Figure 1. John Doe – Leadership Development Plan

Overall Purpose: To build a better relationship with my boss

Developmental Opportunity	*Attitude Adjustments (changes I want to make in my mindset)*	*Visible Behaviors (behaviors clearly evident to others)*
Get aligned with my boss—share his objectives	• I'm not easy to manage; I need to look at my style from my boss's perspective and make adjustments • I need to ground this relationship in a solid foundation of trust • It's my job to support what my boss is trying to accomplish	• Stop debating with my boss in public; take those conversations to our 1:1s • Be open-minded about my boss's requests; ask better questions • Align my work to support his goals; work on things that matter to him • Demonstrate to others that I'm fully onboard with the mission
Repair the relationship—proactively move us to a better place	• I've created a "story" about my boss, one that may not be accurate • I have to improve this relationship — it's my responsibility • Others are noticing my attitude toward the boss; I need to be conscious of how I'm projecting my feelings	• Stop complaining about the boss to my peers • Look at the positives in this working relationship; be objective • Get to know the boss on a personal level; take an interest in him as a person • Tell my boss directly—"I'd like to have a better relationship"
Become a positive supporter—help him succeed	• My success is tied to his; I need to make him successful • There are areas in which I can help him and our group; I need to be less self-centered and see the bigger picture • A positive mindset beats a negative attitude every day	• Spend time with him in non-pressure situations • Give him more positive feedback on his meetings and emails • Stop fighting his style; go with the flow better on his personality quirks • Verbally support him publicly—in our group, and with other teams

noticing? What's working? How is the boss responding? At this point, you need feedback on how you're doing, so don't be shy about asking others for input. The act of documenting your strategy and seeking feedback serves as a catalyst for your ultimate goal—taking responsibility for improving the boss relationship.

Common Boss/Motive Scenarios

While every boss relationship is unique, there are certain boss/motive patterns that I consistently encounter in my coaching practice. The four most common poor-boss profiles I see are: 1) the insecure boss, 2) the ego-driven boss, 3) the control-freak boss, and 4) the career-focused boss. These profiles may seem like broad generalizations, but trust me, these bosses exist. My intent is to give you an overall view of what these bosses want from you, and provide advice for modifying your attitude and behaviors. In doing so, I'll make broad character assessments for the purpose of illustrating the four types; your boss may not fit these exact styles, but some of the motives may look familiar. What I can tell you is that these boss/motive patterns hold up across industry, gender, company size, culture, and level in the organization.

The Insecure Boss

This boss is motivated by fear. He's so insecure about his standing in the organization that he'll do anything not to rock the boat. He won't take risks, and doesn't generate innovative ideas. He's afraid of his boss, and as a result, does whatever he's told to do. He doesn't want you talking to his peers because he's paranoid you'll make him look bad. He won't challenge anything and operates opaquely, with little communication or explanation (he doesn't want you to see how timid he is). In a word, he's worried about his own job security.

What does he want from you? He wants you to lie low and not make waves. He tells you: *Just do your job, and don't ask so many questions.* He wants you to keep your head down, just as he's trying to do. Forget about having him sponsor or showcase you; his whole focus is on just getting through another day. Above all, what he wants is you to not make him look bad; he doesn't want to draw attention to himself in any way. I know this is depressing, but there are a lot of bosses out there who fit all or parts of this profile. So what do you do about it? How do you adjust your attitude and behaviors?

First, help him take calculated risks. Look for places to push him (gently) to take action and show him you have support from other groups to take this leap. Second, talk up his successes and best qualities with others. Like it or not, you are in this together; your reputation is linked to his when it comes to innovation, challenging the status quo, etc. Become his best PR agent and try to influence how others see him. Third, gain his confidence as a sounding board; the more he can talk to you about his feelings and concerns, the better chance you'll have of helping him gain self-confidence. Fourth, connect him to successful leaders around the company. If you have better internal relationships than he does, help him get into some of these inner circles. Finally, develop a running dialogue about the need for your team to gain more traction, deliver more results, take on bigger challenges, etc. Be smart about this, but demonstrate that you're ready to do more, and ask him to trust that the team can achieve bigger things. If he feels your confidence, it might boost his own.

Now, if none of this works, the best advice I can give you is to get away from this type of boss; he is stifling your creativity and stunting your career growth. If he isn't making progress, talk with HR about your circumstances, and work the internal job posting system. If you can't get yourself reassigned to another manager in the company, consider leaving the organization. You can tolerate certain types of bosses, but this style will do nothing for your development or career. This type of boss is a brand-buster, and while it's OK for him to stall his own career, you don't want to go down with him. Find a way to help him or move on.

The Ego-Driven Boss

This boss is motivated by being right—all the time. She is convinced her ideas are best, that she's got the only clear perspective, and that she's the smartest person in the room. She may listen to your ideas, but she's not going to implement them (not without putting her spin on it). She doesn't host brainstorming sessions because she doesn't need them; she's already decided what to do. She doesn't invite input or debate at her staff meetings; she gives orders. Her self-worth is tied up in always having the right answer or always making the right decision. She doesn't want to share the spotlight—her ego won't allow one of her direct reports to get credit for anything. Mind you, she doesn't want to control the entire work process (in fact, execution may bore her) but she will control the direction and the ideas. She likes to win, but for her, winning is about being right.

What does she want from you? First, she wants you to find her ideas brilliant. She wants you to worship her knowledge, wisdom, and expertise. She wants you to appreciate what she's teaching you and to be a willing apprentice. She wants you to be grateful that you're on her team, and while you're at it, tell everyone in the company how awesome she is. Mostly, she wants you to execute—to do, not think. Are you working for this type of boss? If so, what do you do? How do you adapt and thrive?

First, sharpen your skills. Demonstrate that you're worthy of being a thought partner; you'll never get that status if you're not executing flawlessly. Second, try this approach when pitching an idea: Ask her to think about it overnight. One of my bosses, Joe, was a master at this—he ended every suggestion by saying: "I just want you to think about it; I'll check in with you tomorrow." By deferring the outright rejection of the idea, Joe actually won more points than he lost. The idea might have been tweaked and ultimately owned by his boss, but Joe still got his ideas into the mix (in a subtle, non-threatening way). Third, don't pout if your ideas aren't being heard; keep a level head and keep trying. If you sulk or start complaining to others, she will pick up on your attitude and you'll likely pay for it. Fourth, bring data and context. Show her that you're an organized thinker, too. Raise your game when it comes to judgment, decision making, and idea generation by doing your homework, and then presenting it in a matter-of-fact way. A smart boss respects and values other smart people; polish your ability to prepare evidence-based assertions and raise your game when it comes to thinking strategically.

Finally, modify your story a bit. She might have a huge ego, but you may be learning a lot from her, and that's valuable to your career. She also might be right about a lot of things, and that is good for your team's reputation. So while you may not enjoy her obnoxious style, the end result is better than working for the insecure or control freak manager. Vow to take away the best parts of working for her. After all, the way she's treating you isn't personal, it's just her style. Label it, understand it, and adapt to it. You might find the advantages of being part of a winning team outweigh the (temporary) lack of appreciation for your own ideas.

The Control-Freak Boss

This boss is motivated by—you guessed it—having complete control. Unlike the ego-driven boss, he isn't the smartest person on the team, and may even be a bit insecure, which is why he wants to control every detail of your work. He's got a Ph.D. in micro-management. He needs to know everything that's going on. He doesn't want you talking to his boss or peers because he wants to control those conversations. Every idea must be vetted, every presentation reviewed, and every step in the process scrutinized. Why? Because he feels that's the only way the work will get done right. He's more focused on process than he is on big ideas. He doesn't lead, inspire, or coach; he *manages*—you and your work. And he does it relentlessly, day in and day out.

What does he want from you? He wants you to follow his direction without challenging it. He wants you to do what he tells you to do. He doesn't want you straying from the plan, and certainly doesn't appreciate you talking with other departments (without his knowledge). Yes, he wants you to execute, but only if you do it his way. You're basically a cog in his machine. He isn't going to give you exposure across the company because he's all about being the indispensable one. He wants you to fly in formation and do your job, not think outside the box or draw attention to yourself. How do you connect better with this type of boss? How do you get aligned?

First, take a deep breath and try to relax. This is the most hard-wired of all the difficult boss types (his motives may drive his non-work behavior, too). This boss is really not going to change; the control gene is too deeply embedded. So modify your story. This is about him, not a reflection on you. Besides, if you're talented, you're not going to work for this type of boss for long because you won't put up with it. Second, in terms of practical adjustments, start by asking permission to do things differently. That's right, literally ask: *Do you mind if I try another solution as well?* Be calm and patient, but start to chip away at his micro-managing. Third, don't challenge him in public because that's a direct threat to his style. Make your suggestions behind closed doors, one-on-one. Fourth, try the direct approach. Talk about his style and how you're struggling with it (again, do this in private). Say: *Jay, I don't feel like you're empowering me to use my creativity. I have a lot of experience I'm not being allowed to use because you want things done a certain way. I'm feeling a bit stifled by your management style; can we work together to allow me more latitude in how things get done?* I believe this is a risk worth taking with the control-freak boss. If you're good, he'll be afraid of losing you, so try this tactic if you've earned his trust and respect.

I find that many people never try the direct approach—simply talking about their issues with the boss. More often than not, when they do, they tell me it works. It takes courage, but I recommend trying it if all else has failed. Becky took this risk. In a moment of raw honesty, she told her boss, "I'm uncomfortable around you. You make me nervous, and I don't think you see my best work as a result. How can we change that?" I was proud of her. She put the essence of their relationship right on the table and invited him to create a mutual solution. It worked; the boss told Becky he was sorry she felt that way, and they put practical behaviors in place to take that awkward feeling out of their relationship. Of all the direct approaches I recommend, confronting the control-freak boss is by far the most common. Practice your pitch with a trusted peer and give it a shot; if you're beyond frustrated with this type of boss, what have you got to lose?

The Career-Focused Boss

This boss is motivated by advancement. She will do anything to get ahead in the company. She's totally focused on her next promotion, and spends most of her time managing up. She's obsessed with power and is ultra-competitive; she doesn't always play nice with her peers and isn't above doing something shady to get ahead. She's not execution oriented, she's outcome oriented—whatever makes her look good. She likes to keep score and openly compares herself (favorably) to other executives. She's not paying much attention to you or your development because she's focused on herself.

What does she want from you? She wants you to make her look good. She wants you to help her get that next promotion. She doesn't want you to steal the spotlight, nor does she want you getting more attention than her, so she wants you to keep a low profile. She's not in this role for the long term, so she's not going to provide a lot of coaching and development. She wants to win (which by itself isn't bad) but she may ask you to do things you're uncomfortable with. She definitely wants you to work hard, because she wants to add your results to her scorecard. She also wants your best ideas—she's going to keep you hidden anyway, so the more good ideas you generate the better she looks. What do you do with this type of boss? How do you take responsibility for making the relationship work?

First, make her look good. Yes, that's right, play along. If you help her get promoted, you'll either get rid of her as a boss or you'll go along for the ride (possibly getting promoted yourself). I know it can be frustrating to work for a corporate climber. They don't give you much attention or focus on your development, but hopefully it's temporary. Recognize her motives and put your shoulder to the wheel. Help her get where she wants to go by giving your all; chances are she will remember you when she's finally in the role she's been chasing.

Second, craft a story about her that will work for every situation. Make it bland, something you can repeat over and over like a mantra. Andy was a sales manager who did this beautifully. Andy's standard boss story was this entire statement: "Pat has been Pat for a very long time." That was it. That was the phrase Andy used (every time) when talking about his boss. Of course, it had a double meaning, and everyone got the joke. With this simple statement, Andy was saying: *Yes, Pat is managing up and cares only about getting promoted, but we aren't going to change that. It is what it is.* This is a subtle but important point: find a way to give your opinion about the boss that won't get you in trouble. If you want to craft it so people recognize that you understand what's going on, fine. Just keep it simple and non-threatening.

Third, don't do anything even remotely unethical. Do not cut corners or enable her misguided judgment. Know your own values and the company policies and insist on doing what is right. Push back if she asks you to do something that is out of bounds. Talk to human resources if it's getting messy; you don't have to assist her in pursuing results that may be tainted by wrong-doing. Have the courage to stand up and say no if she asks you to do her dirty work.

Finally, focus on your own relationship-building skills. This type of boss may crash and burn; they often make enemies up, down, and across the company because people resent their single-minded approach. This is when you need other sponsors and mentors, people who will look out for you if this ends badly. Don't tie yourself to her career exclusively; it might veer off course and leave you scrambling for a foothold in the organization.

These four boss types are the most common ones I encounter in my coaching practice, but there are unlimited variations out there in the workplace. So what is your boss's particular combination of preferences, values, and behaviors? How would you describe her motives? Do you understand all of these factors so you can maximize the relationship? Take the time to work through the recommended questions and exercises in Steps 1 and 2, and then formulate a new plan of action. The most important thing you can do is take responsibility for the relationship; if you can write and communicate a new story, you have a good chance of positively changing your work life.

AFTERWORD

Your relationship with your boss matters—a lot. It's the most critical factor in your engagement and enjoyment of the job. If you have a great boss, he's motivating you to work hard, develop your skills, and thrive in the role. However, if you have a bad boss, he's likely the cause of your frustration, disengagement, and stress, and he probably isn't getting the best out of you. Even if you have a great boss, you're not guaranteed a career full of them; sooner or later, you're bound to work for one you're having a hard time getting along with or figuring out. What are you prepared to do about it?

I believe you need to be the catalyst for improving this relationship. You don't have to be a victim—you can proactively change your attitude and behaviors. Start by studying your boss to really understand his motives. That will help answer the key question, *What does he want from me?* Next, take an honest look at how he sees you and be prepared to incorporate that perspective into your plans for change. Review the exercises in the resources section and actually work through them to document your insights.

Then, armed with these reflections, rewrite your story and adjust your attitude. Try new behaviors and stop destructive ones. Maybe you need to be bolder or softer. Maybe you need to challenge more, or challenge less. Perhaps you need to check your own ego to fit in better with his style. The point is to figure out what your boss really wants from you and try harder to make it all work. By the way, this process takes time, so don't give up after a week or two; keep at it. You need to let your boss adjust to your new attitude and behaviors. Remember, you didn't get to this place with your boss overnight; you're certainly not going to repair the relationship in just a few days. You'll have to be dedicated and consistent with your new story and new behaviors.

Ultimately, you might decide to move away from this boss. That's certainly a legitimate option. In fact, it's become a bit of a cliché; people leave bosses, not organizations. But how many times can you just walk away? What about your next boss? What if he's just as bad, or worse? That's why I believe your best course of action is to try working more effectively with your current boss. The process described in the book is a practice you can use your entire career. Why not start now?

You can do this—you can change your relationship with your boss. But you have to make it happen. Taking the initiative is the toughest part. I know you want the boss to change. I know you want him to make the first move, to say: *Gosh, I'm really sorry I treated you so poorly all these years so I'm going to make up for it.* I wouldn't sit around waiting for that to happen. He's not going to change or adapt to your style; you need to adjust to his. You must look at this relationship differently, and take responsibility for improving it. You can make a more enjoyable work experience for yourself, one where you're working more productively with the boss. But you have to put in the work, and commit to a new mindset. I hope you'll use this book as a road map for that journey. Good luck … I know you can do it!

RESOURCES

The 15 Insight Questions

Study Your Boss

1. What is he like at his most approachable?
   Choose the best interaction plan.
2. What is his preferred management style?
   Adapt to his preferred work style.
3. What behaviors does he reward?
   Stick to behaviors he finds appropriate.
4. What is he trying to accomplish in this role?
   Consider his views on your function and his mission.
5. What is he worried about?
   Always know his priorities.
6. What is his reputation in the company?
   Be aware of his leadership brand.
7. Whom does he respect?
   Know who he respects and why.
8. Where does he have influence?
   Remember, his level of influence impacts you.
9. What's his relationship like with his boss?
   This is a major driver of what he wants from you.
10. What is his primary motivation?
    The single biggest indicator—what really drives his behavior?

Consider How Your Boss Sees You

⓫ What does she value about you?
Know how she views your skill set.

⓬ How vital are you to her mission?
Stay relevant to her agenda.

⓭ What does she think you need to improve?
Know what she really wants you to work on.

⓮ How does she represent you to others?
Be aware of her sponsorship and support.

⓯ What is her history with you?
Consider where you've been before determining where to go.

THE REFLECTIVE EXERCISES

Study Your Boss

❶ **Keep a daily diary of your boss's moods.**

To-Do: For a month, document his moods and connect them to his actions.

Action: Use this knowledge to approach him when he's most receptive.

❷ **Document his dominant work style.**

To-Do: Capture his preferred work style—how does he like to manage the work?

Action: Adapt your attitude and behaviors to his style; he's not going to change it for you.

❸ **Make a list of your boss's preferences.**

To-Do: Document behaviors that your boss rewards and punishes, then make a do-and-don't list.

Action: Behave accordingly and try to hit his positive reward buttons.

❹ **Determine his mission in this role.**

Action: Write it out—what is his view of your field or function?

To-Do: Align yourself with his mission; if you can't get aligned, ask to discuss the issue.

❺ **Document his top priorities.**

Action: Write down his top 3–5 priorities; what is he currently focused on?

To-Do: Assess where you fit into these priorities, then either relax or step up your game.

❻ **Articulate your boss's leadership brand.**

Action: Capture your boss's dominant leadership traits—how do people describe him?

To-Do: Be aware of how others view your boss and build your own relationships at his level.

❼ **Make a list of whom he respects and why.**

Action: Create a "boss relationship map"—where does he have strong or shaky relationships?

To-Do: Use this knowledge to navigate the organization to your advantage.

❽ **Assess who and what he's able to influence.**

Action: On the relationship map above, indicate whom he effectively influences.

To-Do: Leverage that influence where you can, but establish your own brand where he struggles.

❾ **Be aware of how your boss talks about his boss.**

Action: Make a list of the words he uses to describe his boss.

To-Do: Be aware of this dynamic, and establish your own relationship with your boss's manager.

❿ **Determine your boss's primary motive.**

Action: Write a description of your boss's primary motivation.

To-Do: Use this single motive to create an overall plan for working more effectively with your boss.

Consider How Your Boss Sees You

⓫ Make a list of your strengths.

Action: Document 10–12 of your best skills and capabilities.

To-Do: See your strengths from your boss's perspective; which of your skills does she fully utilize?

⓬ Compare your priorities to her overall goals and objectives.

Action: Capture her top goals and objectives; circle the ones you're directly involved in.

To-Do: Use this analysis to get a sense of your importance to her mission.

⓭ Document your "unspoken" development opportunities.

Action: Make a list of the behaviors your boss wants you to work on but won't share with you.

To-Do: Follow your instincts; start working to improve in these areas.

⓮ Determine where you rank among your peers.

Action: Write a description of your boss's ideal employee, then rank order her direct reports.

To-Do: Where are you on her "favorites" list? What can you learn from those above you?

⓯ Plot the history of your relationship.

Action: Draw a horizontal line; place positive events above the line, negative ones below the line.

To-Do: Use this graph to study the history of your relationship; look for critical incidents.

ACKNOWLEDGMENTS

Several people contributed to the writing of this book, and I'd like to thank those who inspired me and offered ideas and encouragement. First and foremost, my wife Maureen provided guidance and patience throughout the writing process, and read the manuscript many times to help me get it right. Maureen, thank you for listening and making suggestions along the way, and thanks for helping me keep this work in perspective.

Next, I'd like to thank the amazing staff at Berrett-Koehler, most notably Neal Maillet and Jeevan Sivasubramaniam. As editor, Neal provided countless suggestions and helped me shape the structure and theme of the book. Thanks Neal, for believing in the book's purpose, and helping to make it a reality. As managing director, Jeevan drove the entire publishing process, ensuring that I got valuable feedback and making it easy for me to hit my deadlines. Thanks Jeevan, for your expert stewardship.

Next, I want to thank all of my former bosses. I learned something from every boss, whether we were perfectly aligned or struggling to understand each other. Working for both great and difficult bosses helped shape my views of this critical work relationship and the process presented in the book. Looking back, I only wish I had applied the process more rigorously with certain bosses!

Finally, I want to thank my coaching clients. While I've not used their real names throughout the book, their stories are real. It takes courage to make this process work, and I appreciate these leaders being open to the challenge. Thanks for letting me facilitate your development journey; it's truly been a privilege.

INDEX

ABOUT THE AUTHOR

Steve Arneson is a nationally recognized speaker, executive coach, and leadership consultant. He founded Arneson Leadership Consulting in 2007 to provide practical solutions for individuals and companies looking to enhance their leadership impact. Prior to that, Steve served as the head of leadership development and talent management at divisions of PepsiCo and Yum Brands, and later at AOL, Time Warner Cable, and Capital One.

Steve has been named one of America's "Top 100 Thought Leaders on Leadership" and one of the country's "Top 10 Leadership Consultants" by *Leadership Excellence* magazine. As a speaker and seminar leader, Steve has inspired thousands of leaders worldwide to take charge of their own development, working with the principles in his first book, *Bootstrap Leadership*. Steve holds a master's degree in psychology from the University of Kansas, a Ph.D in industrial/organizational psychology from the University of Tulsa, and a leadership coaching certificate from Georgetown University. Steve lives with his family in Boulder, Colorado, and can be reached at steve@arnesonleadership.com.

Berrett-Koehler is an independent publisher dedicated to an ambitious mission: *Creating a World That Works for All*.

We believe that to truly create a better world, action is needed at all levels—individual, organizational, and societal. At the individual level, our publications help people align their lives with their values and with their aspirations for a better world. At the organizational level, our publications promote progressive leadership and management practices, socially responsible approaches to business, and humane and effective organizations. At the societal level, our publications advance social and economic justice, shared prosperity, sustainability, and new solutions to national and global issues.

A major theme of our publications is "Opening Up New Space." Berrett-Koehler titles challenge conventional thinking, introduce new ideas, and foster positive change. Their common quest is changing the underlying beliefs, mindsets, institutions, and structures that keep generating the same cycles of problems, no matter who our leaders are or what improvement programs we adopt.

We strive to practice what we preach—to operate our publishing company in line with the ideas in our books. At the core of our approach is stewardship, which we define as a deep sense of responsibility to administer the company for the benefit of all of our "stakeholder" groups: authors, customers, employees, investors, service providers, and the communities and environment around us.

We are grateful to the thousands of readers, authors, and other friends of the company who consider themselves to be part of the "BK Community." We hope that you, too, will join us in our mission.

A BK Business Book

This book is part of our BK Business series. BK Business titles pioneer new and progressive leadership and management practices in all types of public, private, and nonprofit organizations. They promote socially responsible approaches to business, innovative organizational change methods, and more humane and effective organizations.

A community dedicated to creating
a world that works for all

Dear Reader,

Thank you for picking up this book and joining our worldwide community of Berrett-Koehler readers. We share ideas that bring positive change into people's lives, organizations, and society.

To welcome you, we'd like to offer you a free e-book. You can pick from among twelve of our bestselling books by entering the promotional code **BKP92E** here: http://www.bkconnection.com/welcome.

When you claim your free e-book, we'll also send you a copy of our e-newsletter, the *BK Communiqué*. Although you're free to unsubscribe, there are many benefits to sticking around. In every issue of our newsletter you'll find

- A free e-book
- Tips from famous authors
- Discounts on spotlight titles
- Hilarious insider publishing news
- A chance to win a prize for answering a riddle

Best of all, our readers tell us, "Your newsletter is the only one I actually read." So claim your gift today, and please stay in touch!

Sincerely,

Charlotte Ashlock
Steward of the BK Website

Questions? Comments? Contact me at bkcommunity@bkpub.com.

OTHER A TO Z GUIDES FROM THE SCARECROW PRESS, INC.

1. *The A to Z of Buddhism* by Charles S. Prebish, 2001.
2. *The A to Z of Catholicism* by William J. Collinge, 2001.
3. *The A to Z of Hinduism* by Bruce M. Sullivan, 2001.
4. *The A to Z of Islam* by Ludwig W. Adamec, 2002.
5. *The A to Z of Slavery & Abolition* by Martin A. Klein, 2002.
6. *Terrorism: Assassins to Zealots* by Sean Kendall Anderson and Stephen Sloan, 2003.
7. *The A to Z of the Korean War* by Paul M. Edwards, 2005.
8. *The A to Z of the Cold War* by Joseph Smith and Simon Davis, 2005.
9. *The A to Z of the Vietnam War* by Edwin E. Moise, 2005.
10. *The A to Z of Science Fiction Literature* by Brian Stableford, 2005.
11. *The A to Z of the Holocaust* by Jack R. Fischel, 2005.
12. *The A to Z of Washington, D.C.* by Robert Benedetto, Jane Donovan, and Kathleen DuVall, 2005.
13. *The A to Z of Taoism* by Julian F. Pas, 2006.
14. *The A to Z of the Renaissance* by Charles G. Nauert, 2006.
15. *The A to Z of Shinto* by Stuart D. B. Picken, 2006.
16. *The A to Z of Byzantium* by John H. Rosser, 2006.
17. *The A to Z of the Civil War* by Terry L. Jones, 2006.
18. *The A to Z of the Friends (Quakers)* by Margery Post Abbott, Mary Ellen Chijioke, Pink Dandelion, and John William Oliver Jr., 2006
19. *The A to Z of Feminism* by Janet K. Boles and Diane Long Hoeveler, 2006.
20. *The A to Z of New Religious Movements* by George D. Chryssides, 2006.
21. *The A to Z of Multinational Peacekeeping* by Terry M. Mays, 2006.
22. *The A to Z of Lutheranism* by Günther Gassmann with Duane H. Larson and Mark W. Oldenburg, 2007.
23. *The A to Z of the French Revolution,* by Paul R. Hanson, 2007.
24. *The A to Z of the Persian Gulf War 1990–1991,* by Clayton R. Newell, 2007.
25. *The A to Z of Revolutionary America,* by Terry M. Mays, 2007.

26. *The A to Z of the Olympic Movement,* by Bill Mallon with Ian Buchanan, 2007.
27. *The A to Z of the Discovery and Exploration of Australia,* by Alan Day, 2009.
28. *The A to Z of the United Nations,* by Jacques Fomerand, 2009.
29. *The A to Z of the "Dirty Wars,"* by David Kohut, Olga Vilella, and Beatrice Julian, 2009.
30. *The A to Z of the Vikings,* by Katherine Holman, 2009.
31. *The A to Z from the Great War to the Great Depression,* by Neil A. Wynn, 2009.
32. *The A to Z of the Crusades,* by Corliss K. Slack, 2009.
33. *The A to Z of New Age Movements,* by Michael York, 2009.
34. *The A to Z of Unitarian Universalism,* by Mark W. Harris, 2009.
35. *The A to Z of the Kurds,* by Michael M. Gunter, 2009.
36. *The A to Z of Utopianism,* by James M. Morris and Andrea L. Kross, 2009.
37. *The A to Z of the Civil War and Reconstruction,* by William L. Richter, 2009.
38. *The A to Z of of Jainism,* by Kristi L. Wiley, 2009.
39. *The A to Z of the Inuit,* by Pamela R. Stern, 2009.
40. *The A to Z of Early North America,* by Cameron B. Wesson, 2009.
41. *The A to Z of the Enlightenment,* by Harvey Chisick, 2009.
42. *The A to Z Methodism,* by Charles Yrigoyen, Jr. and Susan E. Warrick, 2009.
43. *The A to Z of the Seventh-Day Adventists,* by Gary Land, 2009.
44. *The A to Z of Sufism,* by John Renard, 2009.
45. *The A to Z of Sikhism,* by William Hewat McLeod, 2009.
46. *The A to Z Fantasy Literature,* by Brian Stableford, 2009.
47. *The A to Z of the Discovery and Exploration of the Pacific Islands,* by Max Quanchi and John Robson, 2009.
48. *The A to Z of Australian and New Zealand Cinema,* by Albert Moran and Errol Vieth, 2009.
49. *The A to Z of of African-American Television,* by Kathleen Fearn-Banks, 2009.
50. *The A to Z of of American Radio Soap Operas,* by Jim Cox, 2009.
51. *The A to Z of the Old South,* by William L. Richter, 2009.